Monument Conservation
My Experience with the World Heritage Sites of Kathmandu Valley

Monument Conservation in NEPAL

My Experience with the World Heritage Sites of
KATHMANDU VALLEY

Dr. Shaphalya Amatya

Vajra Publications
www.vajrabooks.com.np

Published by

Vajra Publications
Kathmandu, Nepal

in association with

Eco Himal
Panipokhari, P.O. Box 21966, Kathmandu, Nepal
e-mail: office.ktm@ecohimal.org

Distributors

Vajra Book Shop
Jyatha, Thamel
P.O. Box 21779, Kathmandu, Nepal
Tel.: 977-1-4220562, Fax: 977-1-4246536
e-mail: bidur_la@mos.com.np
www.vajrabooks.com.np

ISBN 978-9937-506-01-4

Printed in Nepal

Dedicated to my father
the late Ananda Prasad Amatya,
my Kancha Baa (Uncle)
the late Bhubaneshwar Amatya
&
my youngest brother
the late Sailendra Amatya

Table of Contents

Author's Note

A French writer has described Kathmandu Valley as 'the Florence of Asia, the city of art par excellence'. Indeed, no-where else in the world can one find the concentration of nature, culture, art and tradition that exists in this beautiful valley. In 1979 UNESCO recognized it as a World Heritage Site. Some have even called it the 'Venice of East' – and indeed, the narrow streets with old artistically and architecturally rich houses could certainly once be compared to Venice. But today, Nepal's image as Shangri-La is fast eroding.

In February 2007 I received a letter from Khwopa Engineering College in Bhaktapur requesting me to deliver a lecture on heritage conservation in Nepal. My friend Dr. Susanne von der Heide had asked me to prepare a paper on the subject about a month earlier. From the letter signed by Dr. Rajan Suwal, Principal of the college, I came to know that the college has recently started a Master's Programme in Conservation and Urban Design, with Dr. Susanne organizing the conservation part of the programme.

On the afternoon of 25 February, I went to the college with Susanne. I met Dr. Suwal and other staff and students who were eagerly waiting to hear my lecture on 'Monument Conservation in Nepal: My Experience with the World Heritage Site of Kathmandu Valley'. On that day I had discussions with Susanne and Dr. Suwal on the need for a book on the history and development of heritage conservation in Nepal, particularly the World Heritage Sites of the Kathmandu Valley.

Then in April my Austrian friend, Dr. Kurt Luger, the chairman of Eco Himal, asked me for an article on the World Heritage Site of Kathmandu Valley, for publication in an international book on World

Heritage and Tourism. I immediately thought of my earlier lecture delivered at Bhaktapur, and prepared a fresh article on the subject. Recently when Dr. Luger was in Nepal he confirmed that the book containing my article would appear shortly.

These two events and also the promise of Dr. Luger to help with publication have encouraged me to prepare a new book on the subject. In fact, I have been introducing the subject of monument conservation in the World Heritage Sites of Kathmandu Valley ever since my first book – *'Archaeology in Nepal'*, published in the Nepali language in 1979. In my book *'Art and Culture of Nepal: An Attempt towards Preservation'* first published in 1991 with a second edition in 1999, and another book in Nepali entitled *'Bishwo Sampada; Kathmandu Upatyaka'* or 'World Heritage: the Kathmandu Valley' published in 2001, I focused on the tradition and history of heritage conservation in the Valley. The present work covers the history of monument conservation in Nepal, with a detailed survey of the attempts of both national and international agencies to protect and preserve the World Heritage Site of the Kathmandu Valley.

I joined the Department of Archaeology (DOA) in 1964 and in 1975 was given responsibility for supervising monument conservation throughout Nepal. Then, in November 1992, I was illegally dismissed from the post of Acting Director-General of the DOA for almost four years. Finally, in July 1995 the Supreme Court reinstated me, until my retirement in December 2000.

For more than two decades I had responsibility for heritage conservation in my country. In this book I have tried to document all those events and incidents, the sweet and sour experiences, that I have faced in my long career. This should give the reader insights into the problems and sorrowful conditions of heritage conservation in Nepal, the Kathmandu Valley in particular.

As far as possible, an English version is supplied for every Nepali or Newari word used. Concerning calendars and dates, Nepal Sambat (NS) is generally rendered in Christian era (AD), a difference of some 880 years. The Bikram Era (BS), widely used in Nepal and the Christian era have a difference of 57 years. Where only a year is given in the text – such as 1997 – what is meant is Christian era, AD. Regarding Lichchavi Sambat, which I have mentioned as only Sambat in various places, it has two categories. The one is used before the rule of King Amsuverma and the other was used by Amsuverma for a short period of time. For the first category of Lichchavi Sambat we have to add 76 or 77 years to get Christian Era, and for the next we have to add 500+76 or 77 to get Christian Era.

In writing of the people whose home is the Kathmandu Valley, I have deliberately used the term 'Newa' rather than the often-encountered 'Newar'. I think the word 'Newar' was coined after the Shah conquest of the Valley in 1769.

I would like to thank my friends Dr. Niels Gutschow, Dr. Götz Hagmüller, Mr Erich Theophile, Dr. Susanne von der Heide, Ms. Ludmilla Hungerhuber, and Dr. Kurt Luger for their unstinting help and co-operation. With their permission I have made extensive use of their writings in this book. I also wish to thank my dear wife Madhuri Amatya for her never-ending support and encouragement, and bearing all sorts of torture while I was busy with my laptop. Last but not least, how can I forget my editor Ms. Susan Hoivik and my publisher, Mr. Bidur Maharjan of Vajra Books, my colleagues in the Keshar Mahal Garden of Dreams, Ms. Sirish Bhatt, Mr. Suresh Shrestha, Mr. Suraj Shrestha, and my colleagues in the Department of Archaeology, especially Mr. Om Kumar Shrestha (photographer), for their help and support in bringing out this book. My thanks to you all.

Dr. Shaphalya Amatya
'Kalpa Vriksha', Museum Marg,
Chawani, Kathmandu,
September 2007

Foreword

The UNESCO World Heritage Convention of 1972 has three principal aims: to promote global awareness and appreciation of the importance of protecting the world's cultural and natural heritage; to create recognition of the universal value of this heritage for all humanity; and to mobilize national and international resources for its protection.

More than 830 sites in 138 countries all over the world are now inscribed on the World Heritage List, and their number is constantly growing. Uniqueness, historical authenticity and integrity are basic criteria for inclusion.

The World Heritage Sites of the Kathmandu Valley of Nepal – in this richly-illustrated volume comprehensively presented in cultural-historical perspective for the first time – deserve their place on the List for many reasons. They are true masterpieces of human creativity. They stand as unique testimony to a wide range of cultural traditions and religions. They represent exceptional examples of the architecture of many different epochs and lifestyles. The highly developed architectural art of the royal squares of the three main cities of the Valley – Kathmandu, Patan and Bhaktapur – transports the visitor to a realm of cosmic unity. As the anthropologist Mary Slusser has rightly noted, this is architecture intended to serve both man and the gods. Temples, shrines and landscape blend harmoniously, indicating the way to yet another dimension – a reality not of this world.

With the recognition of the history of the human spirit and its artistic manifestations as 'culturally valuable', a process of sacralization enters the picture. The World Heritage concept creates a 'fixed point', a centre or *axis mundi,* that provides orientation. As underlined by Mircea Eliade, perhaps the world's foremost scholar of mythology and the sociology of religion, the cosmification or sacralization of any area is always a holy act, a consecration. In arranging and ordering space, we replicate the exemplary work of the gods. The sacred fills the world with content, and the sacred is also the central structuring principle of the whole. The human world is the imitation of cosmogony, the exemplary creation of gods, *imitatio dei*.

Almost all World Heritage sites are important symbols of national culture and character. Most are major cultural tourism attractions of their country. Some (such as the Castle of Schoenbrunn in Austria's capital Vienna, the Pyramids in the Nile delta of Egypt, the Great Wall of China, Angkor Wat in Cambodia) are powerfully evocative symbols of national identity, universally recognized.

However, World Heritage is also a vulnerable, non-renewable resource which must be safeguarded, both to maintain its authenticity and to preserve it for future generations. Protection and preservation of these treasures is possible only with the involvement of the local community as stakeholders, owners and custodians of heritage. This approach generally succeeds with World Heritage Sites whose tourism value is recognized and appreciated. But then the question of carrying capacity arises: how many tourists can a given site absorb, without over-exploitation and loss of value? The challenge becomes to find a balance between conservation and consumption, between maintenance and marketing. (And here let me add that marketing must show proper respect for these 'sacralized spaces'.) In addition, it is vital to ensure that the profits from tourism actually contribute to the maintenance and conservation of the site.

World Heritage Sites serve as reference points for the expression of cultural identity. But they also make it possible for us to participate in the historical experience – from own culture, or an alien one – of a once-existing order of things, now far from our everyday world. The past returns: it can be re-assessed, re-interpreted, placed in new contexts and filled with new meaning. In this way, tourism can develop a non-pedagogically motivated didactic, serving as a platform for learning. It is precisely in the possibility of such a cultural product for consumption that the touristic appeal lies.

Those in charge of managing of World Heritage Sites face a dual challenge: they must both market these treasures, and ensure their protection. Many managers see themselves primarily as guardians, and less as promoters of a tourism product. Unfortunately, adequate public funding is not always available for restoration activities. Thus we should note the concept of entrance fees from visiting tourists – as is practised in Nepal – to guarantee the maintenance of centuries-old temples, shrines and pagodas. In this era of globalization, also tourists become involved in ensuring the future of our world heritage. This is indeed both a global and a local responsibility.

Finally, let me congratulate the author, Dr Shapalya Amatya, whose firm expertise and long-time experience have made possible this remarkable volume. With its wealth of culture-historical detail presented in a readily accessible style and the superb photographs, this is a book that should appeal to a wide readership. And let me express our thanks to Susan Høivik, for sensitive editing of the manuscript.

Kurt Luger
University of Salzburg, Austria
Chairman of Eco Himal

1
Introduction

In the Kathmandu Valley, countless religious and secular monuments have been built over the centuries. Excavations at the ancient site of Hadigaon have shown that early buildings were constructed of baked bricks and timber, using mud mortar. As the Kathmandu Valley – indeed, the entire country of Nepal – lies in an active seismic zone, frequent earthquakes have damaged these monuments, to varying degrees. In times when there were fewer structures and less damage, monuments were easily restored. But during the Malla period in the 16th and 17th-centuries, so many edifices were built that the Valley became known as the home of temples and monuments. Ancient inscriptions have recorded many occasions of monument construction and restoration, but rarely mention the details of such repairs and restoration work. Therefore, very little is known about approaches to and techniques of maintenance and renewal of temples and houses in historic times. (Theophile and Gutschow, 2003, p.11).

From the late 18th-century, the Shah rulers and their collaterals (Thapas, Ranas, Basnets, Pandes and others) carried out considerable construction works in the Valley, but they failed to pay proper attention to maintaining the ancient monuments of earlier dynasties. H. Ambrose Oldfield, who was in Nepal during the time of Prime Minister Jung Bahadur Rana (1846–77), noted: 'It is quite different with the Gorkha Government. They take no interest in the Niwar or any other religious festivals, they contribute no money for their support; they sanction their occurrence, but do not actively encourage them. The natural result is, that all the national or Niwar festivals of Nepal have lost a great deal of importance; and though kept up by the Niwars, who are strongly attached to "things as they were", there is not a tithe of the splendour exhibited, nor of the cost expended upon them, which were observed in the time of the Niwar dynasty.' (Oldfield, 1974, p.289). In those days, the same attitude was dominant in the case of monuments as well.

After every devastating earthquake during these two centuries, important changes may have occurred in our monumental heritage. In numerous cases during various later repairs and restorations, we have discovered that either the structures had been badly restored or repaired or even given different shapes. For example, after the earthquake of 1934, many damaged edifices were not restored at all but were left uncared-for or razed to the ground (Shumsher 1991 BS). The bizarrė-looking Fasidega Temple of Bhaktapur Durbar Square is one highly visible example of such neglect after the great earthquake of 1934. The sixth-plinth and stone sculptures guarding its steps are proof that these remains were once the base of a much larger structure. Today, the whitewashed dome structure is nothing more than a shelter for the deity, clearly out of scale compared to the preserved temple-base.

After Nepal became a free and democratic country in 1951, tourism soon became an important component of the economy. Exposure to the international world and the rise of nationalism at home drew the attention of the government toward the preservation and promotion of the country's built cultural heritage.

Anywhere in the world, political and economic changes will automatically bring changes in many other aspects of the country and its society. But the cultural heritage is one aspect which has always some continuity and unbreakable tradition, and it tends to be less affected by upheavals in society. In fact all the components of our cultural heritage are man-made, including our built heritage. Nepal's built heritage or architectural or visual environment is one component of our cultural heritage that has long served to preserve and protect our independent status and individuality. A country protects and preserves its cultural heritage not only for history, art and architecture but also for its own identity, personality and sovereignty. Our monuments are not only brilliant examples of art and architecture: they are also living, functioning entities still used by the people for attaining religious merit and moral satisfaction. Therefore it is the duty and responsibility of our country, our society and each individual citizen to maintain and preserve Nepal's monumental heritage. Our fathers and forefathers who gifted these cultural gems to us would have wished us to add more to our cultural wealth, or at least maintain and preserve them for generations to come. No one has right to deface them, alter them or destroy them. Such destruction might escape legal penalty, but the mental and psychological punishment will endure.

The Kathmandu Valley is the traditional core of Nepalese culture and is widely recognized as the cradle of a great civilization. With a history of more than two thousand years, the beautiful Valley of Kathmandu is home to an exceptional and unique variety of cultural and scenic wealth – indeed, it is a living museum. Mr. Brown Morton III, Chairman of the United States National Committee for the International Council of Monuments and Sites, rightly observed: 'the Kathmandu Valley of Nepal is perhaps the most beautiful place in the world. Hidden deep in the folds of the Himalaya mountains between India and Tibet, this exotic centre of an exotic kingdom, is nearly a perfect synthesis of natural and man-made beauty.' It is also a place where the sharp separation of the sacred and secular, so typical of today's Western civilization, has not yet occurred. A profound spirituality rooted deeply in Hindu and Buddhist religious traditions pervades every aspect of daily life. The combination of the towering snow-capped Himalaya mountains, the rich array of art and architecture epitomized by the dramatic temples that punctuate the landscape like gilded exclamation points and the perfect integration of daily life and prayer make the Kathmandu Valley of Nepal a cultural resource of outstanding significance.' (Prasai, 1981, p.2) An inventory prepared in collaboration with the government under UNDP supervision calculated that 80% of all historic monuments in the entire country of Nepal are to be found in the Valley. The inventory selected and identified 888 monuments and proposed 34 monument zones (small groups of religious buildings) and 32 preservation districts (small villages and town cores) as well as 24 natural preservation districts (peak sites, forests and recreation areas).As this was a selective list, it did not attempt to cover the smaller shrines of lesser historic importance, which in themselves number many hundreds (Nepal & UNESCO, 1975).

Due to their age and other natural and man-made factors, these historical structures are becoming dilapidated. Urban sprawl, indiscriminate use of non-traditional building materials and the impacts of mass tourism are causing concern. Unless a comprehensive programme to conserve Nepal's cultural and natural sites can be undertaken at once, this priceless heritage of mankind will disappear. Some very important steps have already been taken by the government of Nepal and UNESCO. As early as in 1975, the government recognized the importance of the conservation of cultural and natural sites, and included various projects in the development sector of its fifth plan period. A massive programme for restoring the Hanuman Dhokha Palace in central Kathmandu was initiated by the government and carried out with the assistance of UNESCO, UNDP and several friendly countries. Building regulations were introduced in the historical cities of the Valley. In 1974, during the 18th General Conference of UNESCO, a resolution authorizing the Director-General to include the preservation of the cultural and natural heritage of the Kathmandu Valley was unanimously adopted. Following this, an eight-member team of international experts sent by UNESCO prepared a 'Master Plan for the Conservation of the Cultural and Natural Heritage of the Kathmandu Valley'. Recognizing the outstanding universal value of the cultural and natural heritage of the Valley, the team recommended several urgent steps to be undertaken to save this priceless heritage. The Director-General of UNESCO, Amadou-Mahtar M'Bow, made fervent appeals to the international community to provide assistance to Nepal to enable implementation of the Master Plan. In his convocation address in Kathmandu, Mr M'Bow said: 'if the cultural heritage of Kathmandu is lost, it is in reality losing the very heritage of mankind'. Nepal signed the 1972 World Heritage Convention (full title: the Convention Concerning the Protection of the World Cultural and Natural Heritage) in June 1976 during the visit of the Director-General. At the Second General Assembly of the States Parties to the World Heritage Convention, held in Paris in November 1978, Nepal was represented by H.E. Mr. Upraity, Ambassador and Permanent

Representative of Nepal to UNESCO, and Mr. R.J.Thapa, Director-General of the Department of Archaeology, where it was elected to the World Heritage Committee. Only a few months earlier, Nepal had submitted to the Secretariat of the World Heritage Committee in Paris its nomination forms for the inclusion of the Kathmandu Valley and Sagarmatha (Mount Everest) in the World Heritage List. As explained in the nomination form, seven outstanding monuments and groups of buildings scattered throughout the Valley were seen together as a whole, 'the Kathmandu Valley': 'the cultural heritage of the Kathmandu Valley of outstanding universal value is represented by seven monuments and groups of buildings which taken together as a multiple resource display the full array of historic and artistic achievement for which the Kathmandu Valley is world famous. The seven sites include the three Durbar Squares of Kathmandu, Patan and Bhadgaon, the two Buddhist stupas of Swayambhu and Boudhanath, and the two Hindu temple complexes of Pashupati and Changu Narayan.'

Nepal's application was successful, and in 1979 UNESCO formally declared the Kathmandu Valley a World Heritage Site – not only because of its numerous beautiful monuments but also because these are further enhanced by clusters of vernacular houses, open spaces and other edifices like stone waterspouts, open platforms and traditional rest houses. Today, however, this fantastic World Heritage Site has been totally spoiled by the unruly growth of tall concrete structures, the removal of traditional roofs and the addition of further storeys to old buildings, the demolition of traditional houses and their replacement by ugly concrete structures, and the general encroachment of public open spaces and monuments. Until recently it was possible to see such historical gems as the Taleju Temple, Kashthamandapa, Boudhanath and numerous other edifices from a distance, unencumbered by surrounding buildings. The Poet Laureate Bhanu Bhakta once said that Kathmandu was like Alakpuri, or heaven. But where is that heaven now?

For the protection of ancient monuments Nepal has no dearth of laws. According to the Ancient Monument Preservation Act of 2013 BS (amended six times), any monument or monument zone may be declared as a protected monument or monument zone. No one may build any house or any structure in these protected areas without permission from the Department of Archaeology (DOA). Indeed, even line government agencies are not supposed to install telephone or electricity lines, water pipes, or hoarding boards; do road extensions, film shootings; or organizing festivals and functions, etc., without DOA permission. In reality, however, no one seems to care, and the three historical Durbar Squares (Hanuman Dhokha, Patan and Bhaktapur) are over-used by political parties for public meetings and by various organizations for festivals, mass meetings and so on.

In the WHS and Protected Monument Zones (PMZ) no one is allowed to build or dismantle a house without DOA permission – not even remove the traditional *jingitis* roofs, or construct additional floors. But in practice nobody respects the laws. The DOA can only send letters to stop such illegal construction: actual authority to halt and demolish unauthorized structures lies with the Chief District Officer (CDO). There are very few cases in which the CDO has succeeded in using his authority. The law even has a clause that if necessary the DOA can take possession of the building or any structure by giving reasonable compensation. The newspapers have, on numerous occasions, reported that the ministers have spoken out and declared that the government is ready to provide compensation and take possession of those illegal constructions, but to no avail. As mentioned, the legislation exists: the *Nagar Nirman Yogana Karyanoyan Ain* (Town Development Planning and Implementation Act of 1972, the *Nagar Panchayat Ain* (Municipality Act of 1962) and the *Sthaniya Prasasan Ain* (Local Administration Act of 1971) all contain clauses relating to the protection of monumental heritage, but how little they have been utilized can be judge from the reports of the World Heritage Committee and ICOMOS. It was the ineffectiveness and non-implementation of these laws that led to the Kathmandu Valley WHS being declared a World Heritage Site in Danger in 2003.

Lack of proper co-ordination among the relevant authorities and agencies, lack of firm commitments among the leaders of the country and lack of awareness among the people in general about the need to preserve these heritage sites have hampered the protection of the WHS of the Kathmandu Valley. In BS 2041 (AD 1984), for the protection of the architectural environment of all WHS of the Kathmandu Valley, a directive was issued, making it obligatory, when anyone wishes to build a new house or add floors in old house, repair or change the façade of a house, for a review committee consisting of representatives of the DOA, the Palace Maintenance Office, the Town Development Office, the Municipality and Guthi Undertakings to examine the case and give a decision.

During the Panchayat days (nearly 28 years, 1961 to 1989) and then after the Jana Andolan I of 1989 (the advent of new democracy in the country), the government tried to penalize builders for not obeying the law, but unseen pressures have always managed to supersede the decisions of the authorities. Since the seven monument sites of the Kathmandu Valley were inscribed in the World Heritage List in 1979, both the government of Nepal and the international community have made various attempts to help Nepal to conserve, preserve and promote these heritage sites. However, I remember well that for a long time, neither UNESCO nor the World Heritage Committee ever drew the attention of the Nepalese government to the vulnerability of the Valley's Protected Monument Zones in the context of the rapid pace of urbanization and the destruction of ancient urban fabrics. Many distinguished UNESCO personalities, experts and advisors visited Nepal, and in 1979 a Master Plan for the Conservation of the Cultural Heritage in the Kathmandu Valley was launched. The long-term objective was to assist the government of Nepal in the preservation and conservation of the nation's national cultural heritage in such a way as to ensure the cultural environment and living conditions of the people. It also emphasized that the sites and monuments would be developed to the benefit of the local population as well as to encourage tourism. A joint Campaign Review Committee (CRC) was established with UNESCO and international experts and representatives in 1987–88 for monitoring and reviewing this Master Plan. The first meeting of CRC was held in June 1989. At this meeting, repairs and renovation activities in and around Hanuman Dhokha Durbar Square, Swayambhunath, Patan Durbar, Keshav Narayan Chow (today's Patan Museum), the follow-up programme at Bhaktapur, and the restoration and development activities in Changu Narayan and Pashupatinath temples were examined, analysed and reported.

The second meeting of the CRC was held in October 1991. In this meeting, the CRC appraised the conservation activities undertaken by various national and international agencies under this campaign. The CRC was briefed on the restoration of Hanuman Dhokha Palace, Swayambhunath Hill stabilization and conservation work, the restoration of Patan Durbar, the restoration of the palace and historical houses of Bhaktapur Durbar Square, the initiation of conservation activities at Changu Narayan, and the preparation of a preliminary conservation plan for Pashupatinath. The meeting concluded with the following remarks. 'Since the launching of the International Safeguarding Campaign for the Kathmandu Valley, significant preservation works foreseen under the Master Plan have been accomplished, particularly regarding the protection of the selected monuments, and the opening of museums in some of the restored buildings. Over the next two years it will be necessary to determine what further work is required, so that the safeguarding and presentation of the selected world heritage sites can be successful.'

But the honeymoon was suddenly over in November 1992, when some international experts who had come to Nepal for an international symposium on woodcarving conservation raised the alarm on the deteriorating situation of urban fabrics in these sites. After Jana Andolan I (AD 1989) many old houses that had formed part of the old city's landscape and streetscape were demolished illegally and replaced by new concrete structures. Because of the fluid political situation, the Department of Archaeology, the local administrations and the municipalities could not control these illegal construction works. Some of the experts attending the woodcarving conservation symposium decided that Nepal could be a good place for them to cultivate and expand their own international consultancy services. Immediately after returning home from Nepal, these experts began lobbying against the current state of heritage conservation in Nepal. They put pressure on UNESCO /World Heritage Committee and ICOMOS to dispatch a mission immediately to ascertain the status of the World Heritage Site of the Kathmandu Valley. At a meeting of the World Heritage Bureau held in Paris in June 1993, the matter was further discussed, and a joint UNESCO/WHC/ ICOMOS review mission was sent to Nepal. This Review Mission unanimously recommended that the Kathmandu Valley World Heritage Site should be put on the list of World Heritage Sites in Danger; that there should be increased international support for the World Heritage Site by

UNDP and other appropriate organizations; that, in accordance with the request made to the mission by the Prime Minister, there should be a guarantee of a permanent UNESCO presence at the World Heritage Site. Further, that the Kathmandu Valley WHS should be removed from the list of World Heritage Sites in Danger after a period of one to three years and returned to the World Heritage List when a set of 16 conditions (also known as the 16-point programme) had been fulfilled by the Nepalese authorities.

Since 1993, with great patience both UNESCO and the World Heritage Committee (WHC) constantly and continuously alerted the Nepalese authorities, explaining that unless the situation of the World Heritage Site of the Kathmandu Valley were improved and corrected as required by the World Heritage Convention Regulations, the Kathmandu Valley WHS could be put on the World Heritage in Danger List.

At the third CRC meeting, held in 1994, something quite unprecedented happened. Instead of one report on the status of implementation of the Master Plan, three different authorities of the DOA/Nepal presented three different reports. This created confusion because all these reports were, if not contradictory, generally repetitious and irrelevant, and indicated a serious lack of communication and co-ordination among the authorities of the DOA. During this meeting, for the first time, the international members showed their deep concern about the increasing pressures of urbanization on the historic landscape and townscape of the Kathmandu Valley, particularly since the restoration of multiparty democracy in Nepal in 1990–91. They were of the opinion that the DOA could not exert effective control over the enormous increase in new buildings being erected and old ones that were being demolished and rebuilt. As a result, the principal concern about the future of the built environment of the Valley shifted from the maintenance and restoration of individual buildings to a deeper concern about the need to implement effective systems of development control before the character of the WHS was irretrievably lost. The protection of architectural environment or morphology of these heritage sites became the primary concern at that CRC meeting.

Then at its 21st session in 1997 the World Heritage Committee examined the State of Conservation report on the site. In view of the continued deterioration of the world heritage values in the Boudhanath and Kathmandu Monument zones, affecting the integrity and inherent characteristics of the site, the Committee requested the Secretariat, in collaboration with ICOMOS and the Nepal government, to study the possibility of de-listing selected areas within some Monument Zones, without jeopardizing the universal significance and value of the site as a whole. The Committee commissioned a joint UNESCO–ICOMOS–government of Nepal Mission in March/April 1998. According to its terms of reference, it drafted and provided 55 recommendations and a Time-Bound Action Plan to be adopted by the government of Nepal. The Committee also decided to defer consideration of inscribing the Kathmandu Valley site on the List of World Heritage in Danger until its 23rd session.

At the fourth meeting of the CRC, held in July 1999, the members unanimously praised the outstanding achievements that, in close collaboration with UNESCO, Nepal had made throughout the past campaign period. However, they were deeply concerned about the magnitude and challenges of conservation work still to be done inside the Kathmandu Valley. The meeting recommended that a request be submitted to the UNESCO Director-General to recommend to the General Conference to make a fresh motion to extend, enlarge and strengthen current campaign activities towards the safeguarding and promoting of the Kathmandu Valley's cultural heritage, cultural landscape and riverscape, with further resource mobilization and sharing experiences worldwide.

In October/November 1999, ICOMOS dispatched an expert to report on the current state of conservation and the implementation of the 55 recommendations in the World Heritage Site of the Kathmandu Valley. His report was presented to the 23rd session of the World Heritage Committee.

In September 2000 a high-level mission led by the chairperson of the World Heritage Committee, Director of the World Heritage Centre, Prof. Eduard Sekler and the chief of the UNESCO Kathmandu Office and others visited Nepal. They met with stakeholders, including Prime Minister and the King. They insisted that inscribing the Kathmandu Valley site on the list of World Heritage in Danger could be beneficial in terms of mobilizing and directing the attention of the international community towards the conservation and development of the site. But the Nepalese authorities, from the Prime Minister down to a ward member of the municipality, did not appreciate this suggestion. In December 2000, Nepal was invited to attend the 24th General Convention of WHC held in Cairns, Australia. (Incidentally, this was the only convention of the WHC that I attended in my whole career of more than three decades in the DOA – and this was just a few weeks before I was due to retire.) After the Committee presented its report, Nepal was granted a grace period of two years to implement the Time-Bound Action Plan seriously. Nepal was also asked to prepare and launch a Comprehensive Management Plan to improve the conservation situation at its World Heritage Sites, with a special view toward saving their historic urban fabric. At it transpired, Nepal proved unable to preserve the historic urban fabric at most of the sites. And so, at the 27th session held in Paris in June/July 2003, the Kathmandu Valley World Heritage Site was put in the list of World Heritage in Danger.

To our surprise, in March 2001 the fifth CRC meeting was held without fulfilling its earlier commitments. Another shocking thing that happened at this meeting was UNESCO's sudden announcement that it would terminate the CRC as well as its campaign for the conservation of the cultural heritage of the Kathmandu Valley Master Plan. As a consolation to Nepal, UNESCO representative Dr. Hideo Noguchi suggested that a Strategic Action Plan be drawn up, with long-term and short-term goals for the conservation of the cultural heritage of the Kathmandu Valley. However, this was never done. In the meantime – aggravated by various outside factors like the unstable political situation in the country and weak administration at both central and local levels – the lack of public support and tremendous pace of urbanization pressures and, not least, the heavy commercialization of urban space were hastening the deterioration and destruction of the beautiful historical and cultural fabrics of the Valley.

In February 2003, a high-level commission visited Nepal under the leadership of Dr. Tamas Fejerdy, the Chairman of the WHC, as a follow-up of the Cairns decision. This mission recommended that HMG/Nepal enforce laws to prevent encroachment from taking place in the world heritage monument zones. The government must continuously monitor such illegal constructions and make master plans (short-term and long-term) for corrective measures to assure a long-term system for sustainability of the zones and halt the further deterioration of the WHS. Deeply frustrated, Dr Fejerdy noted: 'the beautiful and ancient Kathmandu Valley is in the grip of uncontrolled modernization at the cost of unique cultural heritage it has inherited from the past generations.'

Sad to say, at its 27th session held in Paris in June/July 2003, the UNESCO World Heritage Committee finally included the World Heritage Site of the Kathmandu Valley in the World Heritage in Danger List. This was not a decision taken lightly. Since 1993, UNESCO and the government of Nepal had been trying to improve the deteriorating situation in all the monument zones by implementing the 16-point programme. In 1998, this 16-point programme was expanded into a 55-point programme. But this could not save the ancient urban fabrics in these monument zones. Negligence and inefficiency on the part of those officers responsible for handling the WHS Division in the DOA, and the weak support of local bodies like municipalities and district administrations were mainly responsible for Nepal's humiliation and loss of face in the world cultural community. In Nepal the politicians are quick to make use of conservation issues in their speeches to attract people, but very few are really serious when it comes to action. Enforcement of building regulations is based on political support. Without it, the WHS and other monument zones, areas and sites all over the country are doomed to suffer more. In the five years from 1990 to 1995, the DOA had three different Directors-General.

The decision of the World Heritage Committee/ ICOMOS to put the Kathmandu Valley WHS on the danger list was taken as a great prestige issue by Nepal. By way of appeasement, in autumn 2003 the UNESCO World Heritage Centre sent an expert mission to prepare an inventory of recent constructions and demolitions within Bhaktapur and Pashupatinath Monument Zones and to evaluate the impact of economic and development pressures on the traditional urban fabric of these two zones. This expert mission, led by two experts from Venice, Enrico Fontanari and Giorgio Gianighian, met several stakeholders in Nepal. It was evident that the Nepalese in general had taken the decision of putting the Kathmandu Valley WHS on the danger list as a serious blow to their pride. Therefore in its recommendations to the World Heritage Committee and ICOMOS, the mission clearly stated: 'We must know that the cancellation of the sites from the World Heritage List will imply a much faster erosion of the heritage that could also become a kind of national reprisal against UNESCO. One has to keep in mind that the de-listing, as appeared from most of the speeches and interviews, is felt as a wound to the national pride. Total cancellation would be seriously felt as an offence to the country.' Moreover, they correctly noted that 'a certain degree of alteration is expected in every heritage site in the world, especially in the living city in a developing country's capital city, like Kathmandu conurbation'.

Immediately after the announcement that the Kathmandu Valley had been inscribed on the danger list, UNESCO sent Richard Engelhardt, regional advisor for culture for Asia and Pacific, to console the Nepalese authorities and to gauge the feelings of the intellectuals and general public. He tried to convince the Nepalese authorities that the UNESCO decision should not be taken as a punishment, but rather as a signal indicating the urgency of conservation and commitment for collective effort to prevent further damage.

With the broad objective of getting the Kathmandu Valley removed from the danger list, a technical workshop for the conservation of Kathmandu Valley World Heritage Property in Danger was organized jointly by DOA and UNESCO, 3–7 May 2004 in Kathmandu. In fact this international workshop was held as per the recommendation of the 27th session of the WHC, which had recommended that the state party (Nepal) should legally re-define the core and the buffer zones of all Monument Zones, accompanied by management mechanisms (including legislation) to ensure adequate conservation of the remaining world heritage value of the property in the long term. The committee also indicated the necessity of corrective measures against illegal activities in the future core and buffer zones. The workshop was concluded after drawing up several Action Plans or programmes, to be implemented by 2014. It was also decided that in four Protected Monument Zones (PMZs) –Kathmandu Durbar Square (Hanuman Dhoka), Pashupatinath, Swayambhunath and Boudhanath –provision for two categories, core and supporting area, will be introduced to protect against further damages. The supporting areas (or sub-core areas) will be free from conservation obligations. The PMZs of Changu Narayan, Bhaktapur and Patan will be kept untouched or unchanged.

The majority of participants at the workshop were not in favour of reducing the areas of PMZs. But surely the time has come to re-examine the old demarcations. It would be wise to be rational rather than sentimental. Before the ever-increasing pressures of urbanization damage and destroy the whole picture of our heritage sites, they must be saved. It is always wise not to be over-ambitious – but whatever is decided to be saved should be saved, at any cost. The Nepal government should not delay in launching the approved action plans with the financial and technical co-operation of international agencies, including UNESCO.

International experts agree that in the Kathmandu Valley WHS almost all the monuments are basically in good condition, and once they are restored their state will be much better than before. They also agree that not merely these specific sites, but the entire valley is a World Heritage Site, and that Nepal should control the 'haphazard development' of urbanization. They insist that Nepal should maintain its cultural landscape by minimizing and discouraging a hybridized building culture, and by acting to save the cultural morphology and environment. Admittedly, there are problems with the vernacular architecture located close to the monumental buildings and in areas listed under 'urban fabric'. There has been, and continues to be, unrestrained new construction, often without building permits; the new structures are too high; additional storeys are added to older buildings; and modern building materials are used instead of traditional ones.

Since 1979 numerous UNESCO/World Heritage Centre/ ICOMOS missions have given their recommendations for improving the conditions of our World Heritage Sites and controlling the ever-increasing zeal for demolishing old houses and building concrete boxes. The international organizations do not have any serious complaint against the condition of monuments at these sites, but they have criticized the government heavily for its inability to preserve what little architectural morphology has survived in these sites. Inside UNESCO/ICOMOS, a powerful lobby has remained active against

Nepal's effort to save its World Heritage status. But our friends in international organizations and international INGOs like the Kathmandu Valley Preservation Trust have provided constant support and help in improving and preserving our World Heritage Site.

The government of Nepal has been making serious efforts to save these heritage sites and to implement the recommendations and suggestions of the various international organizations. UNESCO itself became a main catalyst in improving the conditions in the Kathmandu Valley WHS. Then in 2005/06, a major event took place – a new people's revolution, Jana Andolan II. Also during this time of great crisis, the government of Nepal and the people worked hard to prevent further damage and destruction to our WHS. Moreover, within UNESCO/ICOMOS a powerful lobby friendly to Nepal started pleading that if Nepal's demotion to the World Heritage in Danger List were not rectified now, it would bring negative and not positive results, making the situation even worse. As argued by this pro-Nepal lobby, the country had undergone a very big political upheaval, with high hopes but also considerable frustration in the air. If the bad tag were not removed now, the people would become even more frustrated and would not be so keen to preserve the World Heritage sites. If the bad tag were removed, however, the country would take it as a big concession and would be encouraged to take more positive action.

Most recently, a joint ICOMOS/UNESCO mission visited the Kathmandu Valley from 24 to 29 April 2007. In their report to the 31st session of the World Heritage Commission, held in Christchurch, New Zealand, from 23 June to 2 July 2007, they concluded as follows:

> The State Party has continued its strong efforts to establish an integrated management system, continuing to improve coordination efforts for the conservation of this World Heritage property. The mission found the Integrated Management Plan (IMP) now essentially completed, after two and a half years of work, to be exemplary in many respects in addressing the social, political and economic complexities and challenges of this multi-component World Heritage property.(...) the mission reports that the five principal benchmarks for removal of the property from the List of World Heritage in Danger, noted in Decision 30 COM.7A.26, have been met. The mission recommends therefore

the removal of the Kathmandu Valley from the List of World Heritage in Danger. (For complete text, see *http://whc.unesco.org/p_dynamic/sites/passfile.cfm?category=mission_reports&id=8802.*

The IMP was prepared by the DOA in collaboration with the World Heritage Centre and the UNESCO Kathmandu Office. It aims to bring together all stakeholders of heritage conservation, so that future conservation plans and activities can be implemented in full co-operation and understanding. It further envisages educating the local people in heritage conservation and developing greater awareness and consciousness among the general populace. But whether the implementation committee, including all municipalities and other governmental and non-governmental agencies formed under an undersecretary-level officer of DOA, will be effective will be decided by its future role.

Nepal's hopes of regaining lost prestige received a further boost with the visit of UNESCO Regional Advisor, Richard A. Engelhardt. In a press briefing he stated: 'Nepal's positive change has impressed the ICOMOS. The ICOMOS is probably helping the UNESCO remove heritage sites of Nepal from the list of endangered monuments' (quoted in Manandhar, 2007, p.3).

Following the report of the Joint Mission, the 31st meeting of UNESCO/World Heritage Committee and ICOMOS removed the 'in danger' tag, but not unconditionally. The government of Nepal has already agreed to the major pre-condition: that it should immediately launch the Integrated Management Plan and act according to its framework. A five-year period from 2007 to 2012 has been set for seriously implementing the plan. Then in 2012 a Review Committee will examine the overall situation and further steps will be decided. This means that the government of Nepal will have to be very serious and must mobilize public support and international donors in order to complete the IMP within the timeframe allocated.

The most important factor is people's love of their heritage. If they do not think that maintaining and preserving their heritage is worthwhile, then nothing can stop them from destroying it. We need our heritage for protecting and promoting our national identity and culture. We need our heritage for our moral and ethical uplifting. We must always remember that are only the current custodians of a heritage which has been handed down to us by our ancestors. The inclusion of seven monuments sites of the Kathmandu Valley in the World Heritage List has further increased our responsibility, as they are now recognized as the heritage of all mankind. It is our clear duty and responsibility to maintain this heritage so that it can be handed over to future generations. To achieve all these goals, we need international co-operation, backed up by the firm commitment of politicians and officials, and heightened public awareness of heritage preservation. We need good-quality local professionals trained in heritage conservation, new orientations in teaching and researching in conservation science, and very important – the revitalization of traditional craftsmanship, be it brick manufacture and bricklaying, carpentry, woodcarving. All this must build on the people's love of their heritage.

2

History of Monument Conservation in Nepal

According to an inscription at Patan Kumbheshwar temple dated AD 1392, *'Those who repair the wood, stones or bricks of the dilapidated temples of Maheshwar or Vishnu, will be happy and rich day by day, and will ultimately go to Sivapuri or the land of Siva and will remain there happy for ever'* (unofficial translation) (Regmi, 1969, p. 70).

Inter-relations and mutual tolerance between Hinduism and Buddhism as well as the liberal mindset of Nepalese monarchs and the artistic zeal of the people have created an atmosphere congenial to the growth and development of the arts, architecture and culture in the Kathmandu Valley since the days of the Lichchavi rulers in the beginning of the Christian era. What makes the Kathmandu Valley unique is the combination of its magnificent natural environment with its man-made environment, its towns, settlements and cultural sites which are still a part of the living culture, not just remains of a bygone civilization. The Kathmandu Valley, an outstanding open-air museum of unparalleled universal value, is one of the richest cultural treasures of humankind. Each object of art is not only a marvellous creation of human endeavour but also has some history to reveal. The people of the Valley have not only a deep and sentimental attachment to their cultural assets, but they also live and breathe them. That is why the seven important monuments and sites of the Kathmandu

Valley were enlisted in UNESCO's World Heritage List in 1979. (Amatya, 1983, pp.8–14.)

The Kathmandu Valley is a living heritage of mankind, where a remarkable civilization has long been in evidence. Recent archaeological discoveries at Hadigaon in Kathmandu have proved that the Valley was inhabited by a culturally rich people already at the advent of the Christian era. The Lichchavis were among the early settlers; then, from the beginning of the 2nd-century AD, they not only ruled the Valley but also enriched its cultural wealth. The development of art and culture during this period was highly praised by contemporary Chinese travellers and chronicles. The Lichchavis and their allies ruled the Valley till the 15th-century AD. The period after the fall of the Lichchavis till the beginning of the Malla period proper (AD 750–1482) can be termed a transitional period (also known as the Thakuri period). Politically, not much of importance was achieved; but in the field of art and culture it won renown even in the court of Kublai Khan, the great ruler of China and suzerain of the Mongol states of Tibet. Nepalese artists and craftsmen under the leadership of A-ni-ko (AD 1245–1306) travelled to Tibet and China, leaving a deep and lasting influence on the monasteries and temples of Tibet as well as on Chinese temple architecture and iconography. It was during this period that Kathmandu's most impressive pavilion, Kashthamandapa, was built.

The Kathmandu Valley once again gained importance and became a centre of arts and culture during the Malla Period (AD 1482–1768). Like their predecessors, the Mallas proved themselves to be great patrons of arts and culture. At least one modern scholar has said, 'Newar culture rivals that of renaissance Italy' (Coon, 2007, p. 7). Actually, this was more than just a revival of an earlier classical period: a new and very distinct form of the arts and culture developed during the Malla period, easily characterized and recognized for its distinction. With the turn of political events, the centres of administration as well as of art and culture also changed. The Lichchavi period saw the arts and culture flourishing in Kathmandu and Patan, but during the Malla period, all the three Valley cities – Kathmandu, Patan and Bhaktapur – prospered and developed simultaneously. The Malla kings of the three cities vied each other in the development of arts and culture in their respective city kingdoms. What we see today in and around the Kathmandu Valley in terms of cultural heritage and the artistic creations are the enviable contributions of this period.

Most remarkable is the fact that the Mallas gave new lease of life to both Hindu and Buddhist art and culture at a time when these forms were rapidly disappearing from the Indian sub-continent after the advent of the Mugals in the 16th-century AD. Whereas the Mugals and subsequently the British discouraged Hindus and Buddhists from constructing or restoring religious monuments in India, the Mallas not only built them to enrich these two major religions of Asia but also welcomed and provided facilities to those wishing to erect similar edifices in Nepal. As a result, within the course of two hundred years, thousands of temples, monasteries and other architectural gems came into existence in the Kathmandu Valley. Thus the preservation of the cultural heritage of Kathmandu Valley is also synonymous with the protection of Hinduism and Buddhism in the larger context of Asia.

In Nepal, the building of a monument is invariably accompanied with arrangements for its preservation. Conservation is nothing new to Nepalese society. Our ancestors not only built monuments, but also left behind a long tradition of maintaining them through the system of *guthi* (local trusts). Pious Nepalese monarchs and religious-minded individuals established *guthis* for performing socio-religious, socio-cultural and socio-educational activities. The construction and maintenance of a temple, a stupa, a monastery or a *pati* (rest house) had always been supported by the *guthi* system, either in the private or public sector. Our ancestors were well aware that the building of a monument is not complete in itself unless it is provided with proper management for its safety and continued maintenance. To enable the *guthi* system to operate for perpetuity, the founders used to donate some property, either in cash or in kind, generally in the form of cultivable land, to ensure the regular upkeep of the monuments and for the performance of other necessary functions, rites and rituals. The *guthi* has served to underpin cultural continuity in Nepal, and land has been its main resource for centuries (Amatya, 1999, pp. 153–54).

In 1950, political change took place in Nepal. As in every traditional society, these events brought changes in social values. The

Nepalese were exposed to the modern world, and, as a result, they gradually began to compromise their old values. This led to the decline of traditional institutions like the *guthis*. The new generation began to overlook the contributions made by their forefathers to their social institutions. The Land Reforms Act, formulated after 1962, delivered a death blow to this system. Under the *guthi* system, the donated land used to be leased out to farmers upon annual payment in kind or cash. Under the new legislation, farmers were encouraged not to make payment, on the grounds that the tillers were entitled to a major share of the production. As a result, almost all private and semi-private *guthis* found it impossible to function; and gradually began to disappear from the scene. More and more of our monuments were left high and dry. The great earthquake of 1934 and the smaller ones after that in various parts of the country took a very heavy toll. Some structures were rescued and restored, but thousands of others could not be saved. They gradually continue to disappear from the landscape of the country.

Although Nepal has a long tradition of preserving its monumental heritages through the *guthi* system, this is dying out, for many socio-political and economic reasons. Before this traditional system vanishes completely, we should try to save it, because it is a backbone of our culture. Without the *guthi* system, it will be daydreaming to hope to preserve the cultural heritage of Kathmandu Valley in the true sense of term.

Ellen Coon, a researcher of Newa culture, writes: 'I see Tantric Newari Culture being strangled. I can talk on and on about the sad state of Guthi Sasthans and how non-Newar government nationalized all lands endowments that used to fund temples, religious Jatras (festivals). Now it is run exclusively by non-Newars and handled inadequately to say the least and most of the Guthis are dying out slowly' (Coon, 2007, p 7).

In our society, the construction of a monument and its conservation, restoration and renovation have always been practised, as history shows. The visit of the mighty Emperor Asoka to Kapilavastu was marked by the erection of two monolithic pillars commemorating the spots where Krakuchhanda Buddha and Kanakamuni Buddha were born. The pillar inscription of Niglihawa notes that in the fifteenth year after his coronation (i.e., in 255 BC) the Emperor Asoka repaired and enlarged to double the original size the existing stupa of Kanakamuni Buddha. In fact the process of the conservation and preservation of monuments must have gone side by side with the construction of monuments. In the Kathmandu Valley the first settlers – most probably the Lichchavis and their scions – had built numerous edifices, although nothing has survived except some foundations. However, there are numerous inscriptions and records to show that the Lichchavis were very careful and concerned about the conservation and preservation of their monuments. An inscription by King Amsuverma, located at Patan Sundhara and dated 629 AD, refers to the ancient temple of the village of Mating being dilapidated and battered. The windows and the doors of the temple had fallen into decay. Amsuverma helped with the reconstruction of this temple. As there was every possibility of it falling into decay once more for want of proper maintenance, a large sum of money was set apart for the upkeep of the temple. The management of its maintenance was given over to the assembly of Mating village. The Swayambhu Puran refers to the reconstruction of Swayambhunath, the most venerated and one of the most ancient Buddhist stupas in the Kathmandu Valley, by the Lichchavi monarch Brisha Dev.

In the past, maintenance and conservation were highly esteemed socio-religious actions, inextricably built into the lives and rituals of the people. This can be deduced from the forceful references found in ancient Hindu literature and books which guided the social codes and religious mores of the time. In *Manusmriti,* an ancient Hindu text, it is made clear that anyone who damages any temple must restore it at his own expense. Similarly, the great epic *Mahabharata* pronounced a terrible curse upon those who tamper with an endowment for the preservation of any temple or comparable structure. The curse is invoked with equal force in other inscriptions from the very early times. For example, a 6th century AD inscription of Siva Deva and Amsuverma on the premises of the Changu Narayan temple complex says that those who donate land for the maintenance and repair of a *kot* (or fort) will go and live in heaven for 60 years, whereas those who misuse the land, or encourage such misuse, will go to hell for 60 years. Those who seize land donated by themselves or bestowed by others will live in hell as insects.

During the Lichchavi period there were many kinds of *guthis,* such as *Archa Guthi* for making and repairing sculptures. In an inscription at Naxal Narayan Chour of Kathmandu (now kept in the National Museum, at Chawani in Kathmandu), most probably from the reign of King Jayadeva II (AD 713–33), it is clearly stated that the *Betra Daubarika*, or headman of the village, or an important official of the palace should be given 80 Pana Puran (a type of currency) for the maintenance of the chariot, royal palace, etc. Another inscription dated Sambat 455 (AD 532) at Chaitra Sulka Dasami of Pashupati Vasmeshwar erected by Pratihara Dhurba Sangha Barta (an important palace official) states that as a sign of piety and for the benefit of his parents he established a *guthi* under the control of his family members with an annual income of four hundred Nanika Kuta (a type of revenue in kind). This *guthi* was to be responsible for performing daily worship and necessary maintenance and repairs of the five temples to the deities Bhadreshwar, Natheshwar, Suveshwar, Sthieshwar and Ravishwar erected at the Pashupati complex in Kathmandu. Many such examples abound, so it can be safely established that the construction of a monument or a group of monuments was always accompanied by the creation of one or more *guthis*, with independent income-generating means, to ensure continued maintenance.

The tradition of preservation of monuments further developed comprehensively during the Malla period, and countless new monuments of socio-religious nature were also built. The *guthi* tradition based on land revenue started by the Lichchavis became very popular during this period. Thus, throughout the centuries, pious Nepalese rulers and religious-minded individuals established *guthis* for performing various types of socio-religious, socio-cultural and socio-educational activities – and the construction of a monument was certainly a socio-religious and socio-cultural activity. In the course of time, the *guthis* became a main support, the very backbone of the Nepalese cultural heritage.

The tradition of conservation of monuments flourished during the Malla period. The magnificent Swayambhunath Stupa was renovated in the 12th-century by Maitri Chandra Sakya Bhikshu. According to an inscription located at Swayambhu, this *Mahachaitya* (great stupa) had been destroyed by the Muslim invader

Shamsuddhin Ilias in 1349 AD, but it was completely restored in 1372 (492 NS) by Rajharsha Bhallok, the chief state dignitary of Kathmandu, with the permission of King Jayarjuna Deva and his principal aide Jayasthiti Malla. The most venerated Hindu temple, Pashupatinath, was also destroyed by the Muslim invaders but was restored by Jaya Simha Ram Vardan in 1360 AD. In the beginning of the 15th century King Jyotir Malla reconstructed this temple once again. King Bhupalendra Malla had it renovated in 1689, and also reconstructed the temple of Changu Narayan, which had been destroyed by fire. The most famous Malla king of the 17th century Kathmandu, Pratap Malla, restored the temples of Taleju and Pashupatinath. According to 'Siddhagni Kotyahuti Deval Pratistha' a small temple of Nyatapol was demolished and a bigger and larger temple was constructed by King Bhupatindra Malla (AD 1696–1722) on the same site in 1702.

The system of regular maintenance was consistently followed during the reign of the Mallas as well as their successors, the Shahs. Some of these *guthis* still exist, although not in an active form to undertake restoration.

In the Rana period for some years the traditional public institution called *Chhen Bhadel Adda* (office), probably dating from the Malla period, had also been responsible for repairs to ancient and public buildings. It had always been a part of the durbar (Royal Palace) administration. (Parajuli, 1986, p.11)

The Kathmandu Valley suffered from a great earthquake in 1833, which damaged or destroyed numerous monuments as well as private houses. After this earthquake important monuments like the temple of Pashupatinath and Indresvara Mahadev of Panauti were rebuilt. (Wright, 1966, p. 183)

After the Shah conquest of the Valley in the late 18th century, the kings Rana Bahadur Shah and Griwan Yuddha Vikram Shah and prime ministers Bhimsen Thapa and Jung Bahadur restored and reconstructed numerous religious edifices all over the country. They focused especially on structures along the banks of holy rivers, like the monumental edifices along Kathmandu's Bagmati River from Teku Dovan to Thapathali and Pashupati Gauri Ghat to Raj Rajrajeshawari Ghat. It was during the time of Rajendra Bikram Shah in the 19th century that Prime Minister Jung Bahadur had extensive repairs carried out to the steps of Aryaghat and the steps leading to the Guhyessvari temple and the resting places for the dying. Till the earthquake of 1934, the original architecture was normally retained in restoring and repairing temples and other edifices.

After the great earthquake of 1934 Prime Minister Juddha Shumsher restored and reconstructed many built heritages throughout the country. However, to a great extent the original configuration of many monuments was sacrificed: on the one hand, the operation of restoration and reconstruction had to be accomplished as quickly as possible; moreover, it was impossible to provide sufficient numbers of skilled technicians. Consequently, in the name of restoration and reconstruction the monuments were forced to surrender their original, historical configuration. Nor was it possible to restore, repair and reconstruct all the temples and monuments damaged by this terrible earthquake. For numerous less important monuments, a form of shelter was provided by simple roofs. Numerous multi-storeyed temples were transformed into domed structures. The awkward and outlandish domes that we often see surmounting on the framework of a structure originally designed to be a multiple-roofed temple came in the course of repairs executed after the earthquake. Numerous stone shikhara-style temples in the Valley, particularly in Patan, received no help; they remained as ruins for some time and then slowly crumbled and fell. These changes in Nepal's architecture after the earthquake have not only diminished the importance and value of our heritage but also brought disgrace to our national prestige. But we should not totally discredit Prime Minister Juddha Shumsher, who after all did his best to revitalize the many heritage gems that were the victims of the devastating earthquake.

The Malla rulers had established a permanent agency known as Chhen-Bhadel for conducting repairs, restoration and similar such activities in connection with the ancient and public edifices in the country. In the Newa language, *chhen* means 'building' or house' and *bhadel* probably meant 'guard' or 'keeper'. In some way this office for the maintenance of monuments was continued till its functions were transferred to an organization called the Valley Reorganization Committee *(Upatyaka Nirmana Samiti)* in 1956/57. After the establishment of the Department of Housing and Physical Planning or Department of Buildings, this Committee was automatically dissolved. The Department of Archaeology was established in 1952. The *Guthi Samsthan* or Trust Undertaking was set up in 1964. Also after the establishment of these two agencies responsible for the protection, preservation and conservation of cultural heritages of the country, some other government agencies were involved in heritage conservation activities as well. The Ancient Monument Preservation Act 2013 (1956/57) empowered the Department of Archaeology to preserve ancient monuments in the country. Simultaneously the Guthi Samsthan Act 2021 (1964) explicitly states that His Majesty's Government, if it deems appropriate, is empowered to initiate measures and give directions to preserve any house-building structure or any other immovable property or for the benefit of the general public any important house or building structure important from archaeological, historical or architectural viewpoint or to prevent such structure from decay or dilapidation or ruin.

On the occasion of the coronation of the late King Mahendra in 2013 (spring 1956) a committee was formed, *Upatyakanchal Tatkalin Sudhar Samitee* or the Valley Reform Committee, for the repair and restoration of religious and other cultural heritage sites. Within only three years this committee had cleaned and repaired about 78 temples; moreover, numerous rest houses, stone waterspouts and other small shrines and temples were cleaned, repaired and reconstructed. This committee conducted the task of restoration and repair of the monuments throughout the Valley of Kathmandu, but, for want of skilled manpower and technology, the monuments suffered disfigurement and ruination in the name of restoration and repair. Archaeological conservation principles were almost forgotten: concrete, cement, corrugated sheets for roofing and artificial chemical colours were used extensively in monuments, to provide an attractive outward appearance. In some cases the original architecture of the shrines and monuments was totally neglected, leaving a very bad impression. On the other hand, it must be acknowledged that these activities did give a new lease of life to many of our decaying monuments.

In 1967 the Guthi Samsthan and the Department of Archaeology jointly formed a committee known as *Guthi Jirnodhar Tatha Nirman Samitee,* or Guthi Restoration and Reconstruction Committee, under the chairmanship of the Director of DOA. In the course of five years, this Committee restored, repaired and reconstructed about 160 important monuments all over the country. The process of restoration and repair from the archaeological viewpoint was initiated from this period, but due to the lack of skilled manpower, not all operations could be conducted according to strict principles of archaeological conservation.

The majority of ancient monuments throughout Nepal are under the jurisdiction of the Guthi Undertakings. For the Kathmandu Valley, about 85% of the monuments fall within the purview of this organization. After the formation of Guthi Undertakings, some money, however meagre, is spent every year for the restoration and preservation of ancient monuments. Among the most important edifices repaired and restored by this committee are Bagh Bhairav Temple of Kirtipur, Taleju Temple of Patan Durbar, Kashthamandapa of Maru Tole, Bhimsen Temple of Kathmandu, Machindranath Temple of Patan, Kumveshwar Temple of Patan, as well as many others. The Committee has also extended its conservation activities outside the Valley in various districts. However, it does not have among its personnel sufficient manpower with technical competence for restoration and preservation activities. Thus, in a great many cases, in the name of restoration and preservation ancient monuments have suffered and become prone to decay.

In 1966, Kashthamandapa, one of the oldest and most important monuments (by which name the city of Kathmandu was known for many centuries) was restored by the Guthi Restoration and Reconstruction Committee. The antiquity of this monument can be traced from the 12th century, when it is mentioned in a manuscript known as 'Namasangiti'. The ancient kings used the structure as a community hall and a meeting place. Kashthamandapa ('Pavilion of wood'), locally known as Maru-Sattal, is a large wooden pavilion structure with a small shrine to Gorakhanath in the middle. It stands on a square plinth, built of bricks, measuring about 20 metres on each side.

This was the first time in the history of modern Nepal that the restoration of architectural heritage was undertaken on a massive scale in accordance with established principles. The arrangement lasted for some five years before serious difficulties developed, due largely to the problems of dual responsibility, differing aims and objectives of the institutions involved and basic differences in their approaches. After the Guthi Restoration and Reconstruction Committee ceased functioning in 1970, the burden of conservation of monuments fell on the DOA. (For a list of the monuments repaired by the Committee, see Regmi, 1969, pp. 86–87.)

Until the commencement of the fifth Five-Year Plan in 1975, the DOA had been undertaking conservation activities by means of a regular – but sadly insufficient – budget provided by the government. In the Fifth Plan period (1974/75–1980/81) the DOA for the first time was granted a development budget for monument conservation. Since then it has been receiving a development budget regularly, and this has enabled it to conduct more conservation activities. The inclusion of the conservation activities of the DOA in the national development budget was a big achievement, made possible by the cumulative efforts of many national and international agencies and experts. A major milestone in the conservation endeavour came with the preparation and adoption of the Master Plan for the Conservation of the Cultural Heritage in the Kathmandu Valley with the help of UNDP/UNESCO. Since then, numerous monument conservation projects have been running in the country, particularly in the Kathmandu Valley, with the assistance of international donor countries and organizations.

Before the publication of the Kathmandu Valley Conservation Master Plan, the government of Nepal in collaboration with the United Nations and UNESCO prepared an inventory of monuments and sites in 1975. This inventory identified and documented almost all the monuments, shrines, palace buildings and other important edifices of the Valley and categorized 29 historical settlements, 34 monument zones in rural areas and 13 monument zones in the urban area. Roughly 888 individual monuments and cultural sites of immense importance were identified.

As mentioned, the Chhen-Bhadel office of the Malla period continued till the end of the Rana administration in Nepal. Later on it was relocated to the Department of Buildings. This organization was responsible for regular cleaning, maintenance and repair of government buildings and old palaces. As the DOA could not give sufficient attention to the countless monuments and shrines of the

Valley, there emerged the Kathmandu Valley *Nagar Vikas Samitee* in 1976, under the umbrella of the Housing Department, for the protection and preservation of monuments of cultural sites of the Valley, particularly those constructed during the Shah period. This committee did some improvement works at Dharahara, Naxal Nag Pokhari and Ranamukteyshwar temple. But it failed to gain public appreciation; moreover, its approach was not considered to be in line with accepted archaeological principles. It various failures are clearly pointed out in a study conducted by CEDA in 1979, *Kathmandu Valley Town Planning and Its Impact* (Suwal et al., 1979).

Responsibility for the preservation of ancient monuments of remote areas and the Himalayan region was placed with the Remote Area Development Committee constituted under the Ministry of Local Development. Later on the name was changed to *Lama Tatha Gumba Baybastha Samitee,* which means Lama and Monastery Management Committee.

In 1988, under the instruction of the Royal Palace, the Nepal government established *Kathmandu Uptake Samskritik Thatha Dharmik Chertra Bikas Samanoya Samitee* (the Kathmandu Valley Cultural and Religious Area Development and Co-ordination Committee). This Committee, under the management of the Housing Department, was tasked with repairing, restoring and keeping those monuments and temples clean and presentable where once a year the ruling king used to visit. These sites were Daksin Kali, Budhanilakantha, Sheh Narayan, Taudhaha, Changu Narayan, Sankata, Mahakalsthan, Indrayani, Kalikasthan, Bhadrakali, Sova Bhagawat, Maiti Devi, Nara Devi and Naxal Bhagwati.

However, the main burden of monument conservation has lain with the DOA. It is the sole authority in the Protected Monument Zones and the World Heritage Sites. Special units were established to look after the monuments in the three major zones. The Pashupatinath Monument zone is taken care by the Pashupatinath Development Trust. The Changu Narayan Monument zone is under the umbrella of the Bhaktapur Palace Maintenance Office, and Boudhanath is looked after by the Department directly through a Local Development Committee, as in the Swayambhunath Monument Zone.

The heyday of bilateral co-operation in heritage conservation with friendly countries is now over. Some of these countries have continued helping Nepal through the Kathmandu Valley Preservation Trust (KVPT), but lack of support to the KVPT from governmental and other national agencies has discouraged the launching of more ambitious projects. And what of the Nepal Heritage Society, no one knows what it is doing these days? The Ministry of Culture is more occupied with civil aviation and tourism, which now lie within its portfolio. In such a situation what could we expect in the field of monument conservation?

In Nepal it is not easy to trace the original form of any temple or the precise nature of the additions, alterations, or renovations that have been carried out from time to time. If, for example, we take what are arguably the two most important monuments of the WHS – the Pashupatinath Temple and the Swayambhunath Mahachaitya – they have undergone countless repairs, alterations and renovations. This is easily traced by comparing various photographs of those monuments taken in the 19th and 20th centuries.

After the great earthquake of 1934, many monuments were repaired and face-lifted, while less important ones were just given temporary shelters, or even completely removed from the site. As noted by Dr. N.R. Banerjee, 'the extensive repairs that were carried out thereafter to several monuments in Nepal, particularly in and around the Kathmandu Valley, have laudably served to preserve the ancient heritage of Nepal, but often without the essential traces of their ancestral form, leaving to posterity some relics of which the original forms were apparently rather different from what they presently serve to convey' (Banerjee, 1977).

The basic principles of conservation are the same everywhere, though the exact methods employed for conservation or the machinery entrusted with the work may vary from country to country. There is also variation in the types of monuments, the materials used in their construction, and the general state of their preservation, depending upon such factors as age and climate, besides the innate durability of the relics themselves. Each individual situation requires a suitably specific treatment.

As a matter of principle, it is essential that, before repairs to any ancient monument are undertaken; a complete descriptive record of the existing condition of the monument and the proposed repair measures is prepared, and approved by the proper authority. This is to ensure that the architectural character of the monument is retained intact. For this purpose, photographic records of the monuments are also desirable. It may often be necessary to prepare scale drawings of the affected parts of any structure in the form of plans, elevations and section, either in full or in part. These measured drawings alone would enable the executors to carry out the repairs properly and correctly and compare, in the course of checking and as necessary, the condition of the monuments before the repairs with the condition afterwards. Photographs may be useful. These records may help the higher authorities or even responsible members of the public who may find fault with the works of repairs to keep a check on matters and ensure the correctness and propriety of the repairs, if necessary by ordering rectification of any mistakes. (Banerjee, 1977, p. 21.)

The aim of restoration is to preserve and reveal the aesthetic and historic value of the cultural heritage item, by respecting the original materials and authentic documents. As stipulated in the 1964 Venice Charter for the Conservation and Restoration of Monuments and Sites, restoration must not be conjectural, and any new work – restoration of missing parts – must be both harmonious and distinguishable (Articles 9 and 10). Proven modern techniques may be used in cases where traditional technology is inadequate (Article 10). The Venice Charter also says that evidence of all periods of the development of the monument must be respected, and removing this accretion to reveal earlier periods can be justified only in exceptional circumstances and conditions (Article 11). (See Sullivan, 2003, pp. 116–18.)

3

Conservation of Hanuman Dhoka Durbar Monument Zone

Nepal has a lengthy and unbroken history and tradition of cultural heritage. As one of the most spectacular cities inside the Valley, Kathmandu has long been admired and loved by Nepalis and foreigners alike. Located in the heart of the city, the Hanuman Dhoka Durbar, or palace complex, has been especially important – probably the seat of ancient rulers – ever since Lichchavi times, i.e. from the beginning of the Christian era to the 9th century AD. A Lichchavi inscription found in the Degu Taleju temple at Hanuman Dhoka, attributed to King Amsuverma (7th century AD) mentions the restoration of what must have been an older palace. What we do know for certain is that this locality has been the seat of royalty at least since the early 16th century AD.

The Hanuman Dhoka Durbar is designed, like the other royal palaces of Kathmandu Valley, with spacious courtyards surrounded by buildings, temples, gardens and open areas. The palace complex has numerous temples of various architectural styles – pagodas, shikharas, and others. From the beginning of the 16th century to the 18th century it was not only the seat of royalty and administration but also the centre of trade, commerce, arts and culture. As this palace complex has played differing roles in the life of Nepalese royalty and people, a range of various types of buildings have been constructed over the years.

Exactly when the foundations were laid is not known. To judge from available records, King Mahendra Malla (reigned AD 1560–74) can be considered as the pioneer builder. He had numerous temples constructed, inside the palace and in its vicinity. Prominent among these are the temples of Mahendreshwar Mahadev, Chaturmurti Vishnu (the Jagannath temple), Taleju temple, Mul Chowk (courtyard) within the palace – to mention only a few. According to a manuscript from AD 1566, he had Tana Dewal renovated, and offered a gilded roof and a flagpole to the deity. On this occasion he celebrated *Kotyahuti yagna,* the worship of sacred fire, and had the dance drama of the epic Ramayana performed. The Mul Chowk was later restored in AD 1709, during the reign of King Bhaskar Malla.

The Taleju temple was built by King Mahendra Malla in AD 1563. A list complied in BS 1887 (AD 1830) indicates its height as 81 *hat,* or about 40 metres. One of the tallest and biggest temples in the country, it is built atop a plinth of brick. According to religious strictures, no house should be built taller than this temple – but these days no one pays heed. The upper roofs and portions of the temple building were destroyed in the great earthquake of 1934, but were repaired in 1940. Repair works were also carried out by the Guthi Jirnodhar Thatha Nirman Samiti organization, established in 1966.

King Siva Simha Malla (AD 1578–1619) and his queen Rani Ganga Devi were very devout monarchs. Historians have credited them with the renovation of numerous monuments – Pashupatinath, Swayambhu, Changu Narayan, and others. (Munakarmi, AD 1984 (BS 2041), p. 249)

Pratap Malla (AD 1641–74) was one of the most venerated rulers of the 17th century. He not only constructed numerous monuments and new wings in the palace complex but also installed a stone statue of Hanuman (the monkey-faced god) in 1671. Since then the palace has been known as *Hanuman Dhoka Durbar,* or 'the palace guarded by Hanuman'. Pratap Malla and all the Malla kings of Kathmandu after him used this as their official residence, as did the Shah kings until the beginning of the 20th century. Even since then, all major national religious and cultural events of the Shah royalty have been solemnized here.

The Hanuman Dhoka Monument Zone encompasses numerous edifices built by King Pratap Malla. These include the Krishna Mandir, the building around the courtyards of the famous Mohan Chowk, Sundari Chowk, Kabindrapur at Maru Tole, the Indrapur temple, Panchamukhi Hanuman temple of Nasal Chowk, stone pillars with statues, as well as the water garden or Nag Pokhari. Pratap Malla also renovated numerous other monuments, among them Degu Talle and Taleju temple of Hanuman Dhoka, and the Vasuki temple at Pashupatinath. (Munakarmi, ibid, p. 256)

The Queen Mother Riddhi Laxmi had one of the tallest temples in the valley, Maju Dewal, constructed in front of the Gaddhi Durbar at Maru Tole. Also the Queen Mother Bhuwan Laxmi left prominent monuments inside the Hanuman Dhoka Zone: she had Mul Chowk renovated and beautified with two lovely life-size bronzes of the river-goddesses Ganga and Jamuna in BS 1765 (AD 1708).

Records tell us that the main builders of the Hanuman Dhoka complex were the Malla kings of the 17th century, Mahendra Malla and Pratap Malla, and the Shah Kings of the 18th and 19th centuries, notably Prithivi Narayan Shah, Pratap Singh Shah and Rajendra Bikram Shah. The Malla palaces in the three historical cities of the Valley – Kathmandu, Patan and Bhaktapur – were designed and built in more or less the same style of architecture. Then, after the Shah conquest of the Valley, King Prithivi Narayan Shah had the Hanuman Dhoka Palace expanded and further embellished. Two very impressive pieces of architecture, Basantapur and Vilas Mandir, were built during his reign. In fact he only had some upper storeys added, most probably the floors above the height of the palace wing between the Basantapur and Bhaktapur Towers, as well as enlarging the palace area. His son King Pratap Singh Shah had the upper floor of the Vilas Mandir built, as well as three other towers – in the Valley cities of Bhaktapur, Lalitpur (Patan) and Kritipur.

After the Anglo–Nepal war of 1814–16, the ambitions of Nepalese generals became subdued. Political stability was established in the country, providing sufficient time for constructive works. King Rajendra Bikram and his Prime Minister Bhimsen Thapa focused on renovating and beautifying the Hanuman Dhoka Palace and its vicinity. The Bhandarkhal water garden was repaired in 1822, and over the next two years, all prominent courtyards of the palace Mul

Chowk, Mohan Chowk and Sundari Chowk were 'modernized' and renovated. In 1936, the corridors outside the palace were paved with flagstones; three years later, also the Nasal Chowk was paved with flagstones and its historical platform restored.

The Malla palaces of the Valley are surrounded by the temples and shrines of the favourite divinities of the monarchs who had them constructed. They are richly decorated – with monuments, stone pillars with bronze statues of the royal families, a water garden and a stone royal bath, and so on. A garden and a Nag Pokhari (pond with a pillar statue of a serpent god) is another feature. It is said that up to the 17th century the Hanuman Dhoka Palace consisted of 35 courtyards, but now only ten are in existence.

The architecture of this palace complex is both unique and highly complex. The courtyard with four towers in four directions was known as '*Chokuatha*' during the Malla period. Palaces were built in that style because of security reasons. Tall towers in four corners interlinked rooms; small doors and grilled windows are some of the main features of those palaces. These *Chokuthas* are known as the Basantapur Tower, Kritipur Tower, Bhaktapur Tower and Lalitpur Tower.

During their despotic 104-year rule (1846–1950), the Rana prime ministers brought about many changes in the palace complex. During that period the western wing of Nasal Chowk and Sisha Baithak were built in the neo-classical style then popular in Europe. The small doors and windows of the palace were replaced by larger ones. Open verandas and patios replaced the four towers previously connected by terraces. In 1907, after demolishing a part of the old palace, Rana Prime Minister Chandra Shumsher built Gaddi Baithak, which was used till recently by the Shah Kings as a place to receive credentials from newly appointed foreign ambassadors.

Among the three Malla palaces of the Kathmandu Valley, Hanuman Dhoka Palace complex has the most extensive area. It is also large in the scale of its open spaces and structures. It contains about 60 important monuments, most of which date back to the 17th and 18th centuries, in a unique combination of Malla and Shah architectural styles.

The main entrance has a golden gate constructed during the 18th century. Once inside, the visitor comes to Nasal Chowk, the biggest and most used courtyard in the palace complex. The Malla kings used this courtyard for public audiences: here they met the people, listened to their grievances and dispensed justice right on the spot. The courtyard was extensively rebuilt and renovated in the early 19th century by King Rajendra Bikram Shah. Most of the buildings surrounding this beautiful courtyard date from the 18th and 19th centuries. The Shah rulers used the courtyard for celebrating many important social, religious and cultural functions and events. The north wing is known as *Sisha Baithak,* and served as a hall of public audience in old days. The two temples on the right and left of the building are the *Agan Chhen* or sacred temple house, and the Pancha Mukhi Hanuman temple. In the eastern wing of the palace there is a temple to Nrityashwar, the Dancing Siva. The local people call it Nasal Devata – from which name this courtyard became famous as Nasal Chowk. So important is this temple that, ever since the Malla period, it has become a practice that all important religious and cultural functions of the city – especially dance and dance dramas –is to be performed here, to please the god of dance, Nrityashwar.

Next is Basantapur Chowk, also known as Lohan Chowk or the courtyard paved with stone. Four towers of different architectural designs surround this courtyard, with the nine-storey Basantapur Tower on the southwest corner the most magnificent and prominent among them. The tower on the southeast corner is known as Bilas Mandir, or the house of pleasure, or Lalitpur Tower. The northwest tower is known as Bangla or Kritipur Tower, and features a copper roof of unusual design and complexity, the sole example in Nepalese architecture. And finally, the northeast tower is called Laxmi Bilas, or pleasure house of the goddess of wealth Laxmi. The Basantapur Tower and the Bilas Mandir were erected by the founder of the Shah dynasty, King Prithivi Narayan Shah; the other two towers, the Bangla and the Laxmi Bilas, were constructed by his son Pratap Singh Shah in the late 18th century. All the connecting terraces, with artistic wooden windows, can be viewed from this courtyard. Nasal Chowk can be entered from the southwestern side of this courtyard, through a huge wooden gate embellished with beautiful images of the Astamatrikas (Mother Goddesses) and floral decorations.

The rich treasure house of Nepalese art and architecture of Hanuman Dhoka Palace has served various dynasties, kings, and princes. Much of Nepal's history has been written here. This magnificent palace has witnessed many conspiracies, battles, deaths, murders, as well as royal ceremonies, festivals and functions. With the assistance of UNESCO and other donor countries and agencies it was repaired, restored and strengthened in 1975. At the request of the Nepal government, the Hanuman Dhoka Renovation Project was established in 1972 – the first-ever restoration and conservation project launched in Nepal with the financial and technical assistance of UNESCO.

The first phase of renovation activities concentrated on the towers and buildings around the Nasal Chowk – the Kritipur Tower, the Basantpur Tower and the adjoining building. Work was completed in December 1974, in time for the coronation of the late King Birendra Bikram Shah Dev, held in February 1975. For the completion of repair works of this courtyard, besides the UNDP/UNESCO contribution, grants were received from the governments of Nepal, Japan and France, from the Pisa Foundation (Italy) and the Britain–Nepal Society. Part of the local cost was met by a special subsidy from the Nepal Royal Palace.

Stage two, which started in September 1975, involved the straightening of the leaning Lalitpur Tower and repair of the octagonal Bhaktapur Tower. The section of the palace known as the Vilas Mandir, between these two towers on the eastern side of the complex, was also repaired. The German government provided the majority of the funding; further funds were later made available by the Nepal government and UNESCO. Stage three was the most ambitious; it involved the complete repair, renovation and rehabilitation of the Vilas Mandir and the building surrounding the Lohan Chowk.

During the restoration process of the Basantpur Tower, multiple layers of different types of paint were removed from all wooden structures. This led to the rediscovery of superb wood carvings of the Malla period and the early Shah period. The door leading into the Lohan Chowk is one of the largest of its kind, filled with carvings with hundreds of skulls forming a border to the door frame, entwining snakes and a fine carving of the Lord Ganesh over the lintel. Similarly on the lower half of the Basantapur Tower, the most exciting and sensual carvings were exposed – undoubtedly some of the best carving of the Malla period.

As a preparation for starting the restoration in the Basantapur Tower, bamboo scaffolding was erected, which rapidly became a focus of local attention. Thousands of pieces of bamboo were tied with thousands of meters of string, applying a new technique of safety knots. The height of the tower is 30.5 meters, and the topmost roof required major structural repair after being damaged in the 1934 earthquake. A new structural base to the roof was inserted, replacing the old decayed and damaged timbers. The pinnacle and its base measured 4.6 by 1.5 meters and stood 3 meters above the roof. This had to be dismantled and lowered to the ground by means of a homemade block and tackle. It was then repaired and re-erected. The roofs were totally replaced with new timbers and the traditional interlocking joints were then improved. All timbers were also chemically treated for protection against further beetle and fungal attack. (Sanday, 1979, pp. 67–72).

The Kritipur Tower has a Bengali-style roof covered with copper roofing that was originally gilded. Due to poor repairing in previous times, the tower was on the verge of collapse. The generally rotten condition of the timbers used as rafters caused a further weakening of the structure, and as a result of several earth tremors the timber joints had failed completely. Therefore the tower had to be dismantled completely. Detailed documentation and drawings were prepared, and then each structural component was carefully dismantled, recorded and handed over to the carpenters. As every piece of the roof structure was curved and many sections were completely rotten, the first work was to gather pieces that made up at least one quarter of the roof shape so that one could copy exactly and make mirror images of the missing sections. In this way the structure was re-formed and temporarily re-erected to ensure that the pieces fitted together. Perhaps the most arduous task was the preparation of the curved rafters, which all had to be replaced. While the carpenters were working on the repair and replacements of the structure, the carvers were repairing and replacing the damaged sections of carvings. The preparatory work took nearly nine months, and about four additional months were required for the careful fitting together of all the pieces of this major jigsaw. As protection against further timber decay, each piece was dipped in a chemical bath filled with fungicide and insecticide and left submerged there for about two hours. The copper roof posed a further problem. In terms of conservation, the original roof covering should have been put back. But in this case it was considered that the original copper roofing had outlived its use. The old copper sheeting was carefully removed and used as a template for new copper sheets that matched the original in outward appearance and size.

After the earthquake of 1934 the Lalitpur Tower was leaning over 15 degrees from the vertical, as could be seen from a distance. It had not collapsed because, shortly after it was damaged, some engineers (generally said to have been from Germany) propped up the building. When examined for restoration, however, it was found to be in a very dangerous state and had to be dismantled and completely renovated. Due to the considerable movement caused by the earthquake, the structure beneath the tower had opened up enough to allow rainwater to percolate through to the timber supports, causing extensive structural failure almost to the point of collapse. With the judicious insertion of concrete beams and bonders, brickwork to replace the vulnerable timber structure, and having rebuilt the badly damaged north wall, a firm base was provided for the upper section of the Lalitpur Tower. This base was strengthened by the insertion of a concrete ring beam with anchor points onto which the base plate of the windows could be placed. Next, the inner structure was erected, both level and plumb, and to strengthen the framework and prevent lateral weakness. Diagonal bracing, using specially tailored angle irons, was inserted between the vertical posts and fixed horizontal members to form a lattice girder around the upper part of the structure. These braces were bolted together through the vertical posts to give added rigidity, and the whole structure was hidden in brickwork. The roof was replaced using over 90% of the original structural members which had been duly referenced. Various key joints that had become loose were strengthened with iron clamps or braces, and timbers that had been lengthened by using scarf joints were replaced, where possible, using a single length.

Compared to other towers, the repair and conservation of the Bhaktapur Tower was less complicated. The roof, its covering and the carved windows had remained basically intact. The work carried out was of a general nature, involving re-roofing to incorporate new techniques evolved earlier. The complex roof pattern was a challenge to the traditional roof tilers, and their skills were central in enhancing this very decorative and unusual tower.

The next important structure renovated by the project was the west wing of one of the original Malla courtyards, known as the Masan Chowk. This building lies to the west of the Siva-Parbati temple across the main street, and is currently occupied by curio and souvenir shops. The original structure had been badly damaged by the 1934 earthquake. The main wall overlooking the street was sagging in several places and the whole structure was leaning seriously backwards. In many places, the top storey was on the point of collapse, and the bearing ends of most of the floor joists and the timber lintels supporting them were in an advanced stage of decay. As a remedy each joist was removed and a new one was carefully inserted into position. To consolidate the wall and ensure a sound base for the new upper brick wall, the structure was cleverly consolidated with reinforced concrete columns and beams inserted in the thickness of the walls and floors. The building was carefully cleaned of its stucco finish to reveal the beautiful glazed brickwork (Sanday, ibid, pp. 77–78).

The Hanuman Dhoka Renovation Project aimed both at restoring the monumental heritages of the palace complex and at providing a training programme in conservation techniques for administrative staff as well as building craftsmen. The project served as a testing ground for many techniques in repair and conservation, both traditional and modern, and has helped and encouraged Nepalese craftsmen in future conservation activities as well. The reconstruction of the special brick with the co-operation of a traditional brickyard was a major step in saving an earlier craft on the point of extinction. The adaptation of modern techniques for the consolidation of crumbling structures and the introduction of special insecticides, herbicides and waterproofing agents to protect and prolong the life of the fabric of this priceless building are further successful achievements. The project also demonstrated the need for conservation whenever possible, rather than rebuilding, and showed the true value of incorporating reinforced concrete into an important conservation programme. (Sanday, 1978, pp. 168–69). Today the renovated portions also house a bibliographical museum of the Shah monarchs.

The favourable experience of the Hanuman Dhoka Renovation Project inspired local and international support for an integrated conservation programme, which was realized in the preparation of the UNESCO Master Plan for the conservation of the cultural heritage of the Kathmandu Valley in 1977. Repair and maintenance activities have been continuing at Hanuman Dhoka Palace also after the completion of UNESCO project. Restoration, renovation, conservation and other infrastructure development activities inside the palace complex have been made possible thanks to revenues earned by the palace from tourists and shop rentals.

In preparation for the 1989 SAARC Summit, many monuments were repaired and face-lifted in and around Hanuman Dhoka Durbar Square from 1986 to 1988. Funds made available by the Royal Palace and the government enabled repair and restoration work on the ancient Nag Pokhari (pond) and the Siva temple at Bhandarkhal Garden of the Hanuman Dhoka complex. The roofs of important building wings and courtyards were repaired with traditional materials, improving the morphology of the palace square. Flagstone paving was provided all around the famous Trisul Chowk, the biggest courtyard in the palace complex. The architectural condition of the Degu Taleju temple was improved by removing a thick layer of stucco plaster and thereby restoring its original appearance; similarly, the removal of lime plaster or stucco and artificial paints from the woodcarvings restored the original appearance of the famous Kumari Ghar, the house of the living goddess. The physical condition of the building was improved, and the mural paintings inside the main hall of worship were chemically treated and preserved.

Recently, outside the main palace some major monuments have been restored by the Kathmandu Valley Preservation Trust (KVPT), which works to save the extraordinary and threatened architectural and artistic heritage of the Kathmandu Valley. Prominent examples include the 16th century Jagannath Temple, the 18th century Kageswar Temple and the open-air Kal Bhairav shrine. This Trust is currently undertaking the restoration of the Laxmi Narayan temple and the pair of Mahadev temples flanking the entrance to the Taleju

Temple. The Kathmandu Municipal Corporation has restored Maju Dewal, one of the biggest in the square in front of the Gaddhi Baithak. We return to the conservation activities of KVPT and others below.

Judging from a 1830 survey, the Hanuman Dhoka Durbar complex was considerably more extensive than today. There were about 35 courtyards, and even today there are people who remember how the palace complex included the area of what is now a supermarket, Bhugol Park and the Nepal Bank Building, extending up to the New Road Gate. But, after the earthquake of 1934, the opening of New Road and the construction of Nepal Bank building and Jana Sewa Cinema (today a supermarket) severely reduced its territory. Today there are only ten courtyards left within the boundaries of the Hanuman complex.

When the palace complex was included in the UNESCO World Heritage List in 1979, it was listed as including the following major monuments: Nasal Chowk, Mul Chowk, Lohan Chowk, Lamo Chowk, Dakha Chowk, Masan Chowk, Nuchhen Chowk, Kumari Chowk, Mohan Chowk, Trisul Chowk, and Kali Daman Chowk; the prominent roofed temples of Mahendreswar Mahadev, Maha Vishnu Temple, Kotilingeswor Temple, Shiva Kageswor Temple, Taleju Temple, Indreswor Temple, Krishna Temple, Saraswati Temple, Jagannath Temple, Vishnu Temple, Krishna Temple, Siva–Parbati Temple, Maju Dega temple, Maru Ganesh Temple, Bhagwati Temple, Kabindrapur Temple, Trailokya Mohan Temple, Degutale Temple, Krishna Temple and several temples to Lord Shiva. Other monuments include Kampu Kot, Tarani Bahal (or Tana Dewal), Sinha Dhoka, Kal Bhairav Statue, Big Bell, Laxmi Narayan Satan, Kashthamandapa, Singha Satan, Sikan Mugal Bahal, Gaddi Baithak, Hanuman Dhoka (gates), Nautili Durbar, Nag Pokhari, Bandar Khal and Narayan Pokhari.

The small shrine known as the Tana Dewal certainly dates back to pre-Malla times, when it was a shrine of the tutelary deity of the Thakuri kings of Kantipur. As mentioned, King Mahendra Malla had the Tana Dewal renovated and covered its roof with gilded copper, and also offered a gilded flag to the goddess in BS 1623 (AD 1566). An inscription from 1785 says the temple was further renovated by the family of Jaya Pratap Singh Thakul, who had 59 old timber rafters removed and replaced by new ones.

The Hanuman Dhoka Durbar Square is not only a World Heritage Site: it is also the centre of the nation's cultural activities – Indrajatra, Bada Dasain or Durga Puja, Fagu (the festival of colours), and numerous other important religious and cultural festivals and *jatra*s throughout the year. Moreover, the palace square is surrounded by such important monuments as the resident temple of the living goddess, as well as Kashthamandapa (or Maru Sattal), the biggest open rest house and the very landmark of Kathmandu (see below), Simha Sattal, Maju Dewal, the tallest temple in the periphery, Pratap Dhoj or the pillar statue of King Pratap Malla, Taleju temple, and others. No one who visits this palace complex can fail to be impressed by its grandeur and the complex architectural heritage which it represents.

In 1966, Kashthamandapa, from which Kathmandu derives its name, was restored by the Guthi Jirnodhar Tatha Nirman Samiti. The antiquity of this monument can be traced back to the 12th century, as the oldest reference occurs in a manuscript entitled 'Namasangiti' dated AD 1143. Kashthamandapa or the 'Pavilion of wood' is locally known as Maru Sattal, and was used as a community hall and a meeting place by ancient kings. It is a large wooden pavilion structure with a small shrine to Gorakhanath in the middle. This mandap (pavilion) stands on a square plinth, built of bricks, measuring approximately 20 meters on each side. The superstructure resting on the single terraced plinth is supported by four massive wooden pillars of square cross-section, arching upwards to the ceiling. Two successive floors of receding sizes rest on the basic pillars. Wooden staircases ascending from within the inner sanctum provide access from one floor to the other. The façade is enhanced by a wooden balcony with slender carved wooden rails. The beauty of the monument lies in both its simplicity and its dimensions. Kashthamandapa, having passed through many vicissitudes of fortune, commands a pre-eminent place in the history of the nation as a representative of the eclectic and liberal traditions of Nepalese culture. In the architectural realm alone it is outstanding in size as well as antiquity. The *sattal* not only dominated the central town square but stood just beside the ancient trade highway that linked India with Tibet.

Although an 11th-12th century foundation date for the *sattal* can hardly be questioned, certainly the building as it now stands has been restored and renovated from time to time. However, it seems that the basic structure has remained largely intact. The original form of the structure, which had been occupied till 1966 by four or five families who had built their ramshackle shelter inside the shrine all along the façade, with a divers assemblage of materials, had to be reclaimed by the unkind act of uprooting of them from their rather unorthodox and definitely illegal habitat, and by dismantling the structures they had erected. The original lines of the older structure were thus exposed. The worn-out parts of the wooden balconies, and the tiled roofs resting on wooden rafters and purlins, were extensively repaired and/or replaced wherever necessary. Again in 1999–2000 this monument was repaired by the DOA.

In the year BS 2056/57 (AD 1999/2000) the renovation of Maha Vishnu temple of Hanuman Dhoka Monument zone was started and was completed only some three years later. In 2000–2002, some small shrines and temples, including the Kumari Ghar, were repaired.

After the Hanuman Dhoka Durbar Monument Zone was declared a component of the Kathmandu Valley World Heritage Site in 1979, numerous attempts have been undertaken to improve the condition of the individual monuments, but the governmental and non-governmental organizations responsible for maintaining the urban fabrics have not generally had much success. In the years from 1979 till today, numerous vernacular buildings which were a part of the palace architectural environment have been destroyed and replaced by concrete matchbox structures. There is no lack of laws, rules and regulations and even monitoring of the building codes applied in the WHS. But there are always people who try to either misuse or ignore them. On numerous occasions, the government has announced its determination to penalize those who have built without permission. In Hanuman Dhoka Monument Zone there are 79 houses built in contravention of the norms prescribed by the DOA and more than 35 houses built without permission (reported in *Gorakhapatra* daily, 25 Chaitra BS 2058)

As a precautionary measure in July 1984 the Nepal government published a general notice declaring the area included in the World Heritage List as a protected monument zone. But during the 1980s the architectural environment of this palace complex deteriorated to that extent that there was hardly any chance of improvement. On the eastern border in front of the fire brigade but within the monument zone a hotel building was erected, a visual eyesore to the entire area. Similarly on the south of the palace on the way to Jhochen Tole many new concrete buildings have been constructed, and here numerous business and trade houses do lucrative businesses. There existed a medium-sized 18th-century Shah Palace where the new concrete structures appeared just before 1970. Once I visited this palace and could admire a big room covered with most beautiful wall paintings.

As the demarcated area of the WHS was found very limited, it was extended in December 1987. This government notification included some other important monuments, among them the Atkonarayan Temple in the south and Akash Bhairav Temple in the north.

The Atkonarayan temple was built by Queen Ganga Devi, wife of King Siva Singh Malla, in AD 1586. A replica sculpture of Shesh Narayan of Pharping was erected. According to the available records this temple was restored in 1808 and 1919, and most recently in 2002. The Sattal in front of the temple was built by Mathema family of Ombhal Tole in BS 1865 (AD 1808). It was restored in 2007 by donations from members of the Mathema family. Prior to that, it had been personally maintained by Daya Ram Bhakta Mathema.

The Akash Bhairav temple is located at Indra Chowk in the centre of Kathmandu. This unique rectangular temple is one of the most renowned and revered in the Valley – although it does look more like a house than a temple. According to the *Gopalarajavamsabali* (written in the 13th century), in NS 496 (AD 1376) a person named Hari Pandey had the temple corridor paved with stone. Inside the temple, an inscription of King Narendra Malla dated NS 658 (AD 1538) mentions that the king had offered a gilded crown to the deity. This temple was restored or renovated in AD 1909, 1929 and 1939. After the great earthquake of 1934 it was renovated in 1949, and then most recently in 2002. (See Amatya, 2001.)

Here let me relate some of my experiences in the conservation of Hanuman Dhoka Monument Zone. When an old temple-like house with a small temple of Radha-Krishna on the upper terrace in front of the famous Basantapur Tower was being torn down in 1988, the DOA immediately swung into action. After some time, the DOA received the drawings of the new house for which permission had been given by the Kathmandu Municipality. The DOA wrote many times to the Guthi Undertaking to ascertain whether this building was to be a residential one or a temple. The Guthi Undertaking did not give any reply at all. Ultimately the DOA requested the house owner to review and make some changes to the design (in fact, the DOA provided a new, appropriate design to the owner free of cost). The owner was also requested to re-install the deities of the temple as before. The owner finally built the house in a somewhat tolerable design, but without re-building the temple portion. Since then, the DOA has been trying to get the temple re-established. Later on we came to know that that house had been sold to a lawyer.

Another noteworthy case was the house of Harilal and Dhana Maya Bajracharya behind the Big Bell of Hanuman Dhoka. In 1987 the DOA gave permission to Harilal and Dhan Maya Bajracharya to build a house in accordance with the norms prescribed in the protected monument area, and they agreed to construct the house accordingly. However, one year later it was found that the owners were constructing the house according to their own design, totally against the principles set out in the Protected Monument Zone. The DOA repeatedly requested them not to do so and to stop the construction work, but they simply continued. As a compromise the DOA prepared a drawing for the owners to follow, but this they did not accept. Against the DOA's arrest order, the owners petitioned the Palace and continued the construction, committing many follies. They inserted the concrete beams of the new house in the back wall of the historic Big Bell. They raised the height of the house higher than the platform plinth of the Big Bell. They placed cantilevers in the facades, which is also in contravention of the norms. The DOA and the CDO ordered them to demolish all structures which had been built against the prescribed norms. The Kathmandu Valley Town Development Committee also decided to order them to demolish those parts of the building which had been built against the norms and to impose a fine of Nep. R. 6000. But these decisions were not implemented. The owners continued the construction, playing hide and seek with the police and the DOA. The owners did not heed the various government agencies, and completed their illegal construction work in 1989. Today this house stands as a great eyesore to passers-by and a major environmental infraction of the Hanuman Dhoka Monument Zone. (See Tamrakar, 1989.)

Nor is this case unique. Several other highly visible buildings have been built illegally, among them the Suraj Arcade, which lies inside the monument zone. The owner of this Arcade cunningly purchased all the surrounding houses of two big courtyards and demolished them without permission. Then she occupied all the areas including two courtyards and constructed a massive building for a shopping mall. Apparently this Arcade had been granted permission to build up to four storeys, but when the owner tried to construct another floor and increase its height she was stopped from doing so, as the structure lies within the PMZ. When the concerned authorities came to know about these illegalities as well as the impact on the monument zone they requested Kathmandu Municipality and the Kathmandu Valley Town Development Executive Committee to revoke their decisions and withdraw the permission that had been granted. The case was then referred to the Technical Committee for implementing the norms in the monument zones, which recommended a maximum height of 10.7 meters and some alterations to the original design. But the owner did not follow the decisions of the committee and continued construction of the building. The DOA and Hanuman Dhoka Palace Maintenance Office repeatedly sent letters ordering a stop to the construction, but to no effect. Then in 1992, the DOA, Kathmandu Municipality, Chief District Officer's office, District Police and other responsible authorities forced open the upper storey, went on the roof and started demolishing the illegal floor. The assigned height for buildings in the WHS is, as mentioned, maximum 10.7 meters (35 ft), but this arcade building had already exceeded that height. After this action on the part of the authorities, the owner stopped construction. The concerned authorities are still trying to make the façade of the building at least environmentally friendly, but with scant success thus far.

Another case in point is the house of Joyti Tuladhar, just opposite the Suraj Arcade. He was given permission to build a house of five floors – but constructed one with eight floors. When the concerned authorities tried to demolish the illegal extra three storeys, it emerged that he had already filed a case in the court for permission for the sixth one. So, leaving the sixth floor to the decision of the court, the authorities demolished the two uppermost floors. Thanks to this demolition action, the neighbours now have the impression that the government is really serious about protecting the World Heritage Site.

Or take the case of Makhan Tole, where until only a few years ago there were many attractive traditional houses that had been built after the earthquake of 1934. But since Jana Andolan I (AD 1989) many of these vernacular houses have been torn down and replaced by new concrete structures. Seeking to discourage such practices, the government amended and extended the area of protected monument zone 1987, but this could not help to save the old houses. At present on the south of the Suraj Arcade, several houses previously belonging to the Manandhar and Shrestha families have been demolished completely. It remains to be seen what type of building will come there.

Taking advantage of the fluid political situation, particularly during Jana Andolan I and most recently Jana Andolan II (2005/06), many old houses around Hanuman Dhoka and Hanuman Dhoka Monument Zone have been torn down, or their traditional *jingiti* tile roofs have been removed and more floors added. In fact within this monument zone, and more particularly in the surroundings of the palace, there is not a single building where the façade has not been changed, the height increased or open terraces built on the top floor, after the traditional *jingiti* roofs were ripped off. Many new concrete structures have been built, and the heights of the buildings have often been raised. We can see how mercilessly the neighbours have not hesitated even to encroach on the walls and roofs of historical Kabindrapur. Today the famous Kabindrapur and Simha Sattal are surrounded by numerous tall tower-like houses which have been built totally against the law and without proper permission. It is the duty of the Department of Archaeology (its agency in the Hanuman Dhoka area is Hanuman Dhoka Palace Maintenance Office), the Kathmandu

Metropolitan Corporation (KMC), and Chief District Office (CDO) of Kathmandu to execute the Ancient Monument Preservation Act and many other building bylaws. But as the CDO office of Kathmandu is always occupied with a range of other activities, including maintaining law and order in the city, it can hardly find time to devote proper attention to such matters. As a result in a very short time, many ugly structures have mushroomed in the vicinity of Hanuman Dhoka, also inside the monument zone itself. As mentioned, there is no dearth of laws and bylaws for the protection and preservation of cultural heritages including monuments. What is lacking is commitment and sincerity among those responsible for enforcement. According to the Ancient Monuments Preservation Act, the CDO office has power to take action against those who have defied the law. He can order the owner of the house to demolish it and if necessary can send his own personnel to dismantle it, at the owner's expense. But there have been no cases where the CDO has ventured to execute this power. A major factor here is that the people who live in the centre of the city do not show any love and respect for their traditional architectural heritage, but prefer to construct commercially profitable buildings instead.

The renovation of Joshi Agam at Maru Tole is also worthy of note. A report filed by the KVPT to the DOA stated that:

> Documentation prepared for the historic report included photographs of similar Agam buildings in Kathmandu and Patan. This documentation by chance proved useful when the Joshi Agam, which defines the west side of Kathmandu Durbar Square, was partially dismantled and rebuilt with modern fenestration. Our photo remains the only record of the Joshi Agam historical façade and was provided to the DOA and UNESCO World Heritage Centre. Unfortunately, neither of these authorities was able to enforce the rebuilding of the structure in the historical configuration. Though the trustees tried to rebuild this building in traditional style and to a layman it looks quite impressive, it can never be cited as an example of historic conservation. But it can be cited as one of the examples of pseudo-vernacular architecture.

The KVPT has launched 'The Kathmandu Durbar Initiative 2000–2003' in 2000, dividing the Hanuman Dhoka Durbar area into four categories. In 'A' category area it has placed all the northern parts of the palace including Kampu-Kot. In 'B' it has placed all the southern parts of the palace including Maru Tole. The 'C' sector includes areas around Basantapur, and whereas 'D' covers the whole palace including Bhandarkhal Garden. The KVPT recommends giving priority in renovation activities to the monuments around the *Kampu-Kot* area. This KVPT Master plan of Hanuman Dhoka 2000 aims at renovating and improving the area within the space of one decade. One highly commendable activity involved relocating the police office and military barracks inside Kampu-Kot, but in this direction nothing has happened yet. It was announced in the newspapers in Chaitra 7th on Tuesday that the Kathmandu Municipality was ready to hand-over its land at New Road for the police office as replacement. But both the police office and the military barrack are still there. The KVPT has been successfully launching its renovation initiatives, which are undoubtedly provide good examples of conservation works carried out in the Kathmandu Valley WHS (Kathmandu Valley Preservation Trust, The Kathmandu Durbar Initiative 2000-2003, Kathmandu, March, 2000, limited distribution).

The restoration of the Kageswar Mahadev Temple can be cited as one of the KVPT's efforts successful conservation at Hanuman Dhoka WHS.This temple is of prime importance in forming the historic ensemble of Kathmandu Durbar World Heritage Site. It was built by Queen Bhuvan Laxmi, the widow of King Bhupalendra Malla, in AD 1711 in memory of her deceased husband. The principal image, a Shiva Linga made of *asta dhatu* (an alloy of eight holy metals) is housed in the upper-level sanctum. A Guthi was set up by the Queen to perform annual worship in the temple. As in the case many temples funded by royal donations, the significance of this temple – also known as Bhuvanalakshmeswar Mahadev – gradually diminished, as did its religious importance. The structure got its present name, Kageswar Mahadev, after it became a substitute for another religious site, Kageswar Tirtha, located east of the Kathmandu Valley. People come here to pay their respect each year on the day of Bhadra Kagasthami in September/October.

The present shape is not the original one. It appears that the top portion of the pagoda temple constructed by Bhuvan Laxmi was destroyed by the earthquake of 1934 and later rebuilt in shikhara style. The temple, with its juxtaposition of shikhara on arcaded pagoda base, is a fine example of hybrid temple design which emerged during the Rana period. Only two temples of similar forms exist in the vicinity of the Hanuman Dhoka Durbar Square, other one being an unconventional stone temple dedicated to Vishnu, located west of Degutale Temple. This shikhara type of temple form evolved from the Mughal influence in art and architecture. Though small in size, today's Kageswar Mahadev Temple is a crucial part of the historically and architecturally rich square.

In the course of history the temple was dramatically changed, but it still preserves some of the finest and most delicate carvings from the period. The restoration of this temple marked a significant step towards saving a historical monument of the square which was on the verge of collapse. The project was undertaken in a framework which included public outreach activities as well as critical training of manpower in project management, public relations, preservation advocacy and the state-of-the-art conservation technology. Given Nepal's location in a high-risk seismic zone, a vital component of the project involved developing sensitive and effective strengthening measures for retrofitting of the structure. The project was implemented under the full direction and continuous monitoring of key personnel the Trust with collaboration with the Department of Archaeology, Kathmandu Metropolitan City and a steering committee which included community and the government representatives. The restoration of Kageswar Mahadev Temple was made possible thanks to generous support from the US Ambassador's Fund for Cultural Preservation 2004.

Restoration work started in June 2004. The details of the structure were comprehensively recorded in form of digital photographs and ink drawings prepared by the KVPT technical team. A complete set of drawings in 1:20 scale were prepared, including existing ground and first floor plans, principal south elevation and south–north section. Details of the structural as well as other aesthetic elements were photographed. These provided valuable information about the extent and causes of decay in the structure. The detailed documentation aided in determining the numerous factors to be taken into consideration during the restoration process. Typical problems included fragile roof structure, insensitive earlier repairs and damage from monsoon rains.

During restoration, the pinnacle was not touched. In the shikhara, minor repairs were done in damaged portions and whitewashing was carried out. Sections of the parapet wall where cracks had formed were carefully dismantled and redone, with corrections made for improperly executed joints. The roof was redone completely with introduction of a waterproofing membrane (tarfelt) between the planking and the mud layer for protection against rainwater. Old tiles were reused. In windows and timber columns, unsightly red wash was cleaned using water and mild detergent, and missing details and damaged portions were re-carved and re-installed. The damaged *dachi appa* (traditional brick) from the ground floor arcade wall was replaced with new *dachi appa* and done in yellow mud mortar, section by section. The timber plinth beams were replaced with new timbers. The existing carvings on the *lakashi* (base plate or pillar) were replicated in the new ones, and the lost section of the plinth was reconstructed. Together with reconstruction of the east section, damaged veneer bricks were replaced with traditional *dachi appa* laid on the yellow mud mortar, filled *ma appa* (large traditional brick) to create a solid core. The steps were reconstructed with *dachi appa* done in mud mortar.

In the south–north section of the temple, damaged floor tiles were removed. Seepage of rainwater into the core structure was controlled by laying waterproofing tar felt between the tiles and floor. Proper drainage of rainwater was made possible with introduction of copper pipes for outlets from the terrace. On the staircase, the lower four steps had to be reconstructed because they had completely worn out. An entirely new roof was restructured, incorporating new rafters, purlins, eavesboard, wall plates and planking with a waterproofing membrane of multiplast between the mud bed and planking. Steel membranes were incorporated through concealed bolting and steel angles at critical joints, and bolting of the wall plates while retaining the visible traditional timber peg connection. When the paint from the roof struts was removed, damaged and termite-infested timber was revealed. The existing struts were replaced with new plain timber. The wall supporting the roof structure was completely reconstructed using traditional *dachi appa* and *ma appa* brick. The damaged brick from the ground floor arcade wall was replaced with new *dachi appa* done in yellow mud mortar, section by section. Since the beams were in fair condition, they were re-used, after the red paint had been removed. Steel membranes were introduced to stabilize the structure. Non-historic brick-on-edges paving was replaced with traditional timber planking on the arcade, and damaged stone slabs from the lower plinth were replaced with new dressed stone. (For further details, see Ranjitkar et al. 2005.)

Another good example of a restoration project carried out by KVPT is the Indrapur Temple, a traditional two-tiered Shiva temple constructed in about 1764. It is built on a square base with an additional structure adjoining the central sanctuary. Simple carved struts support the upper balconied roof in unique form, completely open, with an extraordinary shape in comparison to typical temples.

During restoration, the existing foundations of pagoda temples were investigated and analysed for the first time in Nepal. It was found that the depth and width were unequal. To protect the structure from further damage as per the suggestion of a seismic engineer, Mathias Beck of Robert Silman Associates, New York, a concrete ring beam was introduced at the foundation level. Gaps between the foundation walls were filled with the same material (brick and mud mortar) to ensure that the entire core would have the same mechanical properties, resulting in homogeneous behaviour during a seismic event.

To strengthen the Indrapur Temple against earthquakes, Robert Silman Associates launched the idea of an independent interior frame made of reinforced concrete. This frame would require a new foundation mat below the existing foundation wall, bracing the temple against the lateral loads induced by a seismic event. If such a design were applied, the temple could withstand an earthquake. This was clearly the best possible solution. However, in order to save historical fabrics *in situ*, we chose another approach and used a reinforced concrete ring beam (30x50cm wide) around the outer foundation walls, tying them like a belt. The ring beam was carefully installed without damaging the historical wall, designed with the full base shear in one direction, so that in the event of a seismic movement the walls will not drift apart.

The existing timber beams that carried the upper walls of the second floor were partly damaged and in poor condition. These beams were supported with steel channels running on both sides, protecting the outer brick wall above the timber arcades. The wall was completely reconstructed using traditional brick in mud mortar at the ground level as well as the first floor outer wall. Four load-bearing timber posts were replaced on four corners of the ground floor wall. The lower roof was completely reconstructed using new *(sal)* timber members. The middle core wall, which bears the load of the upper tower, was in relatively good condition. It was repaired and strengthened for stabilization. On the ground floor, new traditional *(telia)* tiles were paved in lime and *surki* (brick dust). A new drainage system was installed as well. The interior walls were re-built with traditional brick methods to match the original. On the first floor one level above the arcade, new planking was laid to the joist.

The upper tower of the Indrapur Temple collapsed in the great earthquake of 1934. During the repair, the former shape of the upper structure was completely changed. Several photographic records made it possible to restore the tower to its historical configuration, but there were no close-up photographs to identify the details. Reconstructed was carried out with new carvings and timber components based on visual documentation of other buildings from the same period. Restoration work was started in May 2001 and completed in September 2002 just before the annual Indrajatra festival. (Ranjitkar & Roka, 2002)

The Jagannath Temple, a particularly outstanding edifice of the Hanuman Dhoka Palace complex dating back to the 16th-century, has been recently restored. The KVPT is currently renovating the Laxmi Narayan Temple and two small Mahadev temples flanking the main entrance of the Taleju Temple.

After the Jana Andolan II (Popular Revolution) of 2005/06, the physical condition in many parts of these palace buildings has deteriorated to such an extent that once again considerable amounts of money and materials will be required to bring them back into original shape. When I observed the buildings and temples from the highest plinth of the Taleju Temple in March 2007, I noted that many roofs have been destroyed by monkeys and are now exposed directly to the sun and rain. If the Palace Maintenance Office does not take immediate remedial action, the monsoon rains will certainly destroy them. The condition of Mohan Chowk and Sundari Chowk is even more pathetic, and immediate rescue action is imperative.

Recently I also studied one of the most impressive monuments of the Hanuman Dhoka Durbar complex: Kabindrapur, built by no other than King Pratap Malla. The building was dedicated to Nirteshwar or Nasadyahan, and houses images of various deities. The sanctum has two levels of dedication, the upper one to Bhavanisankara and the lower one to Balabhadra, Subhadra and Purusottama. Nrtyesvara and Nrtyesvari appear only among the ten secondary shrines on the ground floor of the facade. It was renovated only a few years ago by the Hanuman Dhoka Durbar Maintenance Office, but not in a commendable fashion. The building is full of rubbish that was not removed after renovation; moreover, during renovation, when the rear wall and the present upper storey were repaired and replaced, this was not done properly. Even from a distance it is evident that this building has been severely encroached from the north, east and south, where recently constructed buildings have seriously damaged the beauty of these historical surroundings.

The physical condition of the biggest temple in the vicinity, the Taleju Temple, is also worsening day by day, and a severe monsoon could lead to its collapse. The inner portions of the temple are not open to the public. Although the exterior may seem to be in satisfactory condition, the chief priest reports that it is leaking everywhere, and that almost all the plinth structures have multiple cracks.

Developments like these examples from central Kathmandu reflect changes in social topography. Profit-oriented business people acquire properties from less affluent families in these prime areas, and then replace ancestral homes with non-traditional commercial structures. By the summer of 2000, there were five such structures in the Durbar Square area. Although they may appear pleasing to the uninformed, they have dramatically compromised the historical authenticity of the neighbourhood. Numerous examples abound in Patan Durbar Square as well.

Maintenance, conservation and restoration activities need to be carried out on a regular basis. But Nepal has been lacking such awareness, and practice. This is painfully evident in Kathmandu's Hanuman Dhoka Monument Zone, where far too many monuments await regular maintenance, cleaning and repair.

Recently restored Kageswar Mahadev Temple, with Taleju Temple in the background (Photo Januaury 2007)

Shisha Baithak and Pancha Mukhi Hauman Temple (Photo 2007), Hanuman Dhokha Durbar in 1975.

Basantapur Tower and Lalitpur Tower after restoration in 1975.

Overall view of Hanuman Dhokha Durbar in 1975.

International participants at seminar on 'Palaces In Asia' visiting Hanuman Dhokha Durbar Complex, May 1990.

Director-General of UNESCO, Amadou Mahtar M'Bow, at Nasal Chowk, Hanuman Dhokha Durbar, June 1978

Director-General of UNESCO, Dr. Fedrico Mayor, at Nasal Chowk, Hanuman Dhoka, December 1988.

View of Kritipur Tower and Basantapur Tower from Nasal Chowk after restoration in 1975.

Jagannath Temple, Hanuman Dhokha Durbar, after restoration in 2007.

Kageswar Mahadev Temple before restoration in 2007.

Kageswar Mahadev Temple after restoration in 2007.

Kageswar Mahadev Temple after restoration in 2007, Gopinath Temple in front.

Siva-Parbati Temple and other monuments in front of Gaddhi Baithak, Maru Tole during Indrajatra festival in 1911 (from Images of Nepal, p. 65)

Maju Dewal, Maru Tole in 1975 view from the south

Maju Dewal before the 1934 earthquake (Images of Nepal, p. 64)

Inner courtyard north facade of Kumari Ghar, Basantapur in 2006

Restoration of Kashthamandapa (Maru Sattal) in 2003 (photo: Department of Archaeology)

Destruction of monuments around Hanuman Dhokha Durbar in 1934 earthquake.

Monuments around Hanuman Dhokha Durbar prior to 1934 earthquake.

Kal Bhairav Statue before 1934

Kabindrapur under restoration in 1986.

Kabindrapur after restoration in 1986.

Maha Vishnu Temple under renovation by Department of Archaeology, BS 2062 (AD 2005).

Joshi Agan Chhen, Hanuman Dhoka Monument Zone, after restoration of Maru Tole (Recent photo).

4

Conservation of Patan Durbar Monument Zone

Patan, also known as Lalitpur, is famed as the home of fine arts and beauty, one of the three principal cities of the Kathmandu Valley. Patan was planned in the shape of a *Chakra*, the circular disc of the Lord Protector Vishnu, as well as the *Dharma Chakra* of the Prince of Peace, Lord Buddha.

Tradition holds the great Indian Emperor Ashok visited the city in the 3rd century BC. As evidence, there stand four Ashoka-style stupas emplaced in the four cardinal directions. The people of Patan believe that the city and its people are under the protection of Lord Red Machindranath (or Avalokeshwar or *Bunga-Deo)*. The ancient urban centre is dominated by a magnificent cluster of palaces and temples, part of the priceless legacy of art and architecture left by many generations of Malla rulers of the Kathmandu Valley, who reigned from the 13th to the 18th c. AD.

Patan has long been a centre of Mahayana Buddhism. According to available records the monastery known as I-Baha Bahi was constructed in the 15th century AD, and is one of the oldest surviving such structures in Patan. The city is estimated still to have more than 450 Hindu temples and shrines and as many Buddhist monasteries *(vihars* and *bahis)*, as well as numerous stupas, *patis* (rest houses), stone waterspouts (*dhunge-dharas*) and ponds. Therefore, Patan rightly claims to be the cradle of arts and architecture of the Kathmandu Valley.

Patan Durbar Square is a remarkable historic space. More than 30 monuments of different styles, each a masterpiece, are clustered in a small area measuring roughly 160 by 70 meters. A further 30 monuments are located in the immediate vicinity. Dr. Eduard F. Sekler of Harvard University has compared the Durbar Square of Patan to San Marco Square of Venice. According to the renowned French Orientalist M. Sylvain Levi, 'it is a marvel beyond the power of words to tell'. Indeed, Patan Durbar is the most spectacular example of Nepalese architecture in an urban context. The historian Perceval Landon has remarked: 'As an ensemble, the Durbar Square in Patan probably remains the most picturesque collection of buildings that has ever been set up in so small a space by the piety and the pride of Oriental man.' In 1979, Patan Durbar Square was designated as one of the seven UNESCO World Heritage sites in the Kathmandu Valley. It was declared a Protected Monument Zone in 1984, and again (enlarged) in 1996.

Right in the middle of Mangal Bazar stands the famous palace of the Malla kings known as Maningal Rajprasad, or the palace of Maningal, probably built during the Lichchavi period. It is not known under which ruler, or when, the foundations of Patan Durbar were laid. The *Manga Hiti* is from the Lichchavi period, and an inscription of the Lichchavi King Narendra Deva dated Sambat 69 (BS 700, or AD 643) inside Keshav Narayan Chowk of Patan Durbar clearly indicate that this was an important place long before the 16th century, when the present palace building was constructed. Historical evidence proves that there was a royal palace at Maningala (today's Mangal Bazar) before the establishment of the independent kingdom of Patan. It was the seat of administration, and the ruler living there was known as *Maningaladhipati,* or the master of Maningala.

Of the later kings of Patan, Siddhi Narasimha Malla (AD 1618–61), Sri Niwas Malla (1661–85) and Yog Narendra Malla (1685–1706) were responsible for beautifying and adding wings to the palace complex. Today the palace complex consists of only three courtyards – Sundari Chowk, Mul Chowk and Manikeshav Narayan Chowk. The palace complex comprised more than thirty monuments. Another attraction of the Patan palace is that it has managed to retain its original appearance, in comparison to the other two Malla palaces of the Valley. In NS 777 (AD 1657) a severe storm damaged many monuments in Patan, but King Siddhi Narasimha had them repaired in a very short time.

Sundari Chowk (literally: the beautiful courtyard) was built by King Siddhi Narasimha Malla in AD 1627 as a residence for his family. As befitted his name – Siddhi Narasimha – he established two stone images, of Siddhi Ganesh and Narasimha, flanking the main entrance to the courtyard. The architectural grandeur of Sundari Chowk is enhanced by the construction of a sunken royal bath, *Tusha Hiti,* in the middle of the courtyard. The gilded, conch-shaped waterspout is topped by a beautiful bronze image of Laxmi Narayan, and the inner walls of this octagonal spout are decorated with small stones and metal images of various deities. The perimeter of the royal bath is surrounded by a pair of serpents carved in stone. At the entrance to the bath there is a stone slab raised off the ground, which was used by the Malla kings for meditation and prayer. The courtyard is enclosed by a three-storey building with beautifully carved windows. On three sides of the courtyard there are open *dalans* used by the Malla kings to meet visitors, officials and the populace. On four sides of the ground floor of the courtyard there are about seventeen *guyakha* or niches which are decorated with wooden images from Hinduism. The open spaces *(dalans)* have carved pillars as supports. On all the sides of the wooden cornice of the ground floor the names of one thousand Shiva Lingams are inscribed. All the windows on the first and second floors have beautiful carvings. The more than forty eave struts have carvings of various deities of Hindu and Shakta traditions. The three carved windows above the main entrance are especially attractive. Two are made of ivory; the middle one was covered by gold plate but today the gold plate is missing. These windows, and indeed the whole building, are in need of thorough restoration.

In 1997 when UNESCO/Japan Trust Fund Project was preparing documentation at Sundari Chowk, the team discovered 17th-century wall paintings in the parts of the building, which had survived the earthquake of 1934. As the part of this project, a detailed investigation of the structure was undertaken to determine what happened to the courtyard during the disastrous earthquake. The results of this work have shown that the west wing, facing Durbar Square, survived almost intact, whereas the east wing collapsed almost completely, except for the ground floor of the façade. The linking north and south wings each have a similar pattern of progressive collapse towards the east, so the western ends are original while the eastern ends have been rebuilt from the first floor upwards. This courtyard was restored only in 1938, only four years after the earthquake, but the intervening monsoon rains of those four consecutive years caused further damage to the areas of the courtyard which had become unroofed as a result of earthquake damage. All the courtyard buildings and the wall paintings inside them need immediate conservation (see Cotte, 1997).

The construction of Mul Chowk, the main courtyard of this palace, was started by King Siddhi Narasimha Malla in the 17th century and completed by his son, King Sri Niwas Malla. A small gilded temple to honour the *Ista-Devata* (the family deity) was constructed in the centre of the courtyard by Sri Niwas Malla in AD 1666. During the Malla period, all royal functions, ceremonies, rites and rituals including cultural functions were performed in this courtyard. Every year during *Dasain* or Durga Puja, the state festival of Nepal, the goddess Taleju or Tulaja Bhawani is brought here from the main temple for worship, and sacrifices of goats and buffaloes are offered. The building around this courtyard is a low, only two storeys high. Although much altered in recent years, it still retains some of its most precious art objects, including the beautifully carved roof struts depicting the Bhairavs and the Matrikas. There are about forty carved struts and a dozen images of various deities. The two life-size bronze statues of Ganga and Jamuna are among the best examples of Patan's metallurgical excellence. Additionally, the copper plates hanging in the courtyard testify to several very important events of those days. In 1990/91, the DOA undertook some minor repair works in the part of the palace in the north of Mul Chowk, facing the Kumari Chowk.

Between Mul Chowk and Mani Keshav Narayan Chowk is situated a massive three-storey brick temple attached to the palace complex: this is *Degu Talle* or the temple of Goddess Tulaja or Taleju, constructed in NS 761 (AD 1641) by King Siddhi Narasimha Malla. This temple was gutted by fire ten years after its completion, and King Sri Niwas Malla renovated it to its original size. A manuscript dated NS 783 (AD 1663) mentions a massive fire in Patan which destroyed many monuments, and goes on to tell that King Sri Niwas

Malla had them renovated in a very short span of time. The earthquake of 1934 destroyed the Taleju Temple and Prime Minister Juddha Shumsher reconstructed it in 1939. In 2003/4 the roof of this temple was again repaired.

The Keshav Narayan Chowk is the third largest courtyard of the Patan Durbar complex. According to popular tradition, before the construction of Chaukwath Durbar a monastery called Ratnakara Mahavihar or Hakha Bahal occupied the site. Later, when the palace needed to expand, the monastery was shifted to another part of the city and a palace extension was built by King Laxmi Kamadeva (AD 1024–40). It is one of the oldest courtyards of the palace complex, and was famous as the Chaukwath Durbar, which in the vernacular means a palace having four towers in four cardinal directions. Although the date of construction of this courtyard is not certain, it is known to have been renovated in 1674–75. A historical diary of events provides a detailed account of its restoration (see Bajracharya, 1967).

This 'Chowkvatha' palace was used by King Siddhi Narasimha Malla in AD 1631 on the occasion of a feast organized for all sages of the Kathmandu Valley. It is popularly believed that King Yognarendra Malla built this northernmost courtyard, known as Keshav Narayan Chowk. The building was further renovated and decorated by King Vishnu Malla in 1733. It is believed that the king with the help of his subjects rebuilt this courtyard after dismantling the old one within three months (Vajracharya, 1964). In the centre of the courtyard, the god Mani Keshav Narayan is seated with his consort Laxmi in *Samantabhadra Mudra* or embracing posture, wearing a crown of jewels and a necklace of precious gems or *mani.*

King Sri Niwas Malla gave royal patronage to this courtyard and made it the residential quarters of royalty. During his reign the main entrance door and the middle window of the second floor were covered and decorated with gilded embossed copper artwork. The gilded window has an embossed image of the Lord Avalokeshwar – the Bodhisattwa of Compassion and the protector deity of Patan. The gilded main entrance door of this courtyard has a beautiful *toran* or tympanum with an image of the goddess Bhagwati. The inscription on the doorframe indicates that major repair work was done on this gate during the time of Rana Prime Minister Jung Bahadur, in 1854.

As in the Sundari Chowk, also this courtyard has three open spaces on the ground level. The windows and the pillars supporting these *dalans* have beautiful carvings, notably the window in the first floor of the north wing, with the Sun God driving his seven horses. But we do not have any evidence concerning the building in the eastern side of this courtyard.

'Is not it like a piece of heaven?' in these words the court poet Kanu Sharma described Patan Durbar Square in AD 1652, and since then writers have not tired of praising this remarkable historic space. As a supplement to the UNESCO/Kathmandu Valley Master Plan, Prof. E.F. Sekler gave a separate proposal for the urbanistic conservation of Patan Durbar Square, recommending the following measures (Sekler, 1980): Firstly, the declaration of monument zone, secondly, the preparation of a fully illustrated comprehensive scholarly inventory of all monument and movable cultural property in the monument zone, thirdly, preservation of the urbanistic arrangement of the square with its splendid vistas and protection against disruptive new buildings and other additions. He also advised that some very disturbing recent changes, such as the creation of tall buildings and super-elevations on existing building, should be remedied. Additionally, most vehicles should be excluded from the Durbar Square and adequate parking arrangements provided nearby. Finally, official policies, regulations and design standards for the monument zone should be announced and continuously supervised and enforced by the conservator of the responsible authorities.

With the support of Prof. Sekler, an Austrian by birth, the Patan Durbar Conservation Project for restoring and rehabilitating the Keshav Narayan Chowk of Patan Palace commenced in 1983, with financial and technical assistance from the government of Austria. This conservation and restoration project had three objectives: to repair all damages and to protect against future risks of decay and destruction; to rehabilitate the historical design of the courtyard which had changed over many years; and to restore and convert the building into a museum, with a structure adapted to new needs and functions. To reduce the risk of rainwater seeping through leaking roofs and terraces and ground moisture rising in the masonry walls (a perennial risk to the structural materials of timber and brick), damp-proof barriers of water-repellent membranes were introduced under the traditional clay and tile roofs and between foundations and walls. To minimize the risk of damage from earthquakes, hidden concrete ring beams or slabs were inserted in necessary places – a practice introduced in the conservation of Hanuman Dhokha Palace. The original use and outward appearance of the Keshav Narayan Chowk Palace had undergone changes in the course of time. Thus, the aim was to rehabilitate the principal façade and the main courtyard, where possible by referring to documents of the original and historic design dating back to 1734. The top gallery, the roof of the main elevation and the tower pavilions in the corners were completely rebuilt according to photographs taken before the earthquake of 1934.

The rebuilding process for the four façades of the main courtyard proved complicated, because no drawings or photographs were found. Some thirty years earlier, when there was no Department of Archaeology in Nepal, the Public Works Department had been entrusted with the task of repairing the building and adapting it for the purpose of a school. At that time, the balcony running around the whole courtyard received a vertical wooden safety grill from floor to roof height, and the roofs were changed to modern factory tiles – so that the historical character suffered considerably. These large tiles have now been replaced with hand-made traditional ones, but with the design of the balcony and the more recently introduced doors and windows, the restorers-architects had to 're-invent' history, by comparison with similar structures from the same period. Since carpenters and masons well trained in other conservation projects can reproduce historical designs and adornments without difficulty, the front portion and main courtyard of the palace now looks very much as it did some two centuries ago, even though some of the elements and materials are not the authentic originals.

Changing and adding staircases achieved more efficient visitor circulation. Non-bearing partition walls were removed and traditional mud floors were replaced with clay tiles. Lime-*surkhi* (brick powder) plaster was used on the walls instead of the old mud plaster – which is beautiful, but too soft for heavy-duty use within a museum.

Since the east wing had to be totally rebuilt because of its poor condition (it had been already rebuilt after the earthquake of 1934 and thus did not have much historical value), a totally new interior on all three of its floors was created with a modern steel frame roof structure, visible from the inside, while maintaining the traditional shape and tile cover of the roof, recreating the historical Malla period façade towards the courtyard. At the rear of this wing, facing the garden, the neo-classical character of its post-earthquake façade was retained, while some modern and even post-modern elements were added, such as the new staircase window and steel beams and pillars. In renovating the east wing, the architect-restorers and the authorities of DOA did try to follow the Charter of Venice, according to which 'each newly introduced component must bear a contemporary stamp'. The surprising thing is that when they actually did follow this latter doctrine (and with good reason) at the rear portion of the building complex, they were misunderstood by some who thought that the introduction of visible steel beams and pillars in such an historical setting was totally inappropriate. But heritage conservation is always an ideological battlefield of beliefs and doctrines in which the practitioners of this art are exposed to criticism from the public and other experts: for being either too radical or far too conservative (Hagmuller, 1997, pp. 112–18.).

In the 1990s a lobby in the DOA, opposed to the use of modern building materials like cement and steel beams, was encouraged to be more vocal on this issue by some international consultants who were unfamiliar with the nature of the monuments and the hazards these structures have been facing for so long. This anti-cement and steel lobby made it a very big issue, without any know-how, and gave considerable harassment, especially concerning the restoration of Patan's Keshav Narayan Chowk. Indeed, the donor country became so annoyed by this harassment that at one point there was talk of abandoning the whole project without completing it. Fortunately, the situation changed: and the project could continue and be completed, finally becoming today's Patan Museum, which was inaugurated by the late King Birendra on 28 October 1997 at a gala function.

In September 1994, with the co-operation of the DOA, a seminar was organized by UNESCO/Japan Trust Fund Project for Patan Durbar Square on the subject 'Innovative Conservation of Cultural Heritage in Nepal'. Participants discussed various issues relating conservation of monuments, but were unable to reach any conclusions. Their main objective was to criticize conservation and restoration projects in which modern materials (cement, concrete beams, steel plates and various new techniques) have been applied by the DOA and such international experts as John Sanday, Gotz Hagmuller and Niels Gutschow to strengthen the monuments against seismic tremors. Sanday used modern materials in the first-ever UNESCO project at Hanuman Dhokha Durbar in the 1970s. In a press statement released in May 1995 he said:

> Realizing the fragility of most of the materials used in the construction of traditional buildings in Nepal, and having studied carefully the structural integrity and failings of these structures, I came to the conclusion early on that the most logical method of repair and consolidation was by careful and minimal intervention using materials that could make up for failure due to material defects or old age. In some cases the dexterous use of steel could strengthen a failing timber joint; or the use of reinforced concrete, carefully isolated from the historical material, by a neutral membrane, could replace or strengthen wall tops or serve as roof plates acting as ring beam and horizontal stabilizer so essential in any seismic retro-fitting. This technology was developed twenty years ago and became widely used and accepted in the brick and timber monuments on which the Hanuman Dhokha Conservation Project Office was working at that time, throughout Kathmandu, Patan and Bhaktapur, under my guidance. (...) In fact I am somewhat reluctant to support the oft-quoted Venice Charter as suitable guidelines for Asia. Today this charter is somewhat outdated as it was drawn up originally over twenty years ago as a charter for Europe. Australia reacted to the Venice Charter and has now successfully developed its own Burra Charter, which grew out of experiences gained from Venice Charter.

Therefore I think that it is high time for Nepal to draft and adopt its own charter for the conservation of monuments. Nepal should have its own conservation charter, to avoid any further confusions and disputes.

Several wings of the palace (Keshav Narayan Chowk) were dismantled based on the architect's decision that these structures, poorly reconstructed after the 1934 earthquake, disrupted the architectural continuity of the palace complex. Moreover, they were not structurally sound enough to accommodate future museum requirements. The north eastern wing was rebuilt in stages between

1993 and 1997, incorporating as much historic fabric as possible. The work eliminated four modern windows added in the 1950s and reshaped the top floor to accommodate new guest studios. The new roof configuration was loosely based on 17th c. examples. (Theophile & Gutschow, 2003, p. 103)

Much of the restored Patan Museum could have been designed differently in order to preserve more historical fabric than the present configuration. Indeed, the project was condemned and almost shut down by a visiting ICOMOS conservation conference. But the brilliance of the whole, with its mix of modern, historical, fake and authentic fabric has become an undeniable success. Its impact is significant in this region, where historical buildings have only rarely been considered for new or contemporary uses. This is also the first time that Nepalese have seen an historical building artistically presented, and the project has already spawned several other adaptive re-use and repair programmes where historic buildings would otherwise have been lost (Theophile, 2003, p.123).

During the restoration and renovation process, traditional craftsmen and their apprentices received practical on-the-job training. By way of sub-contracting some portions of the work, the project contributed to the timely development of qualified construction firms, specialized in monument renovation. Through preserving a prominent historical monument on a site selected under UNESCO's World Heritage List, presenting and displaying in it one of Nepal's finest art collections, and in the process developing the professional skills required for future conservation tasks, the Patan project succeeded in giving a major boost to local and international efforts for the conservation of the cultural heritage of Kathmandu Valley.

A highly impressive and exquisite monument is the stone temple of Krishna, placed in a commanding position in the Durbar Square complex. King Siddhi Narasimha Malla built this temple in 1636. It features 21 gilded pinnacles – the most ever made in the Valley. Another unique feature of this temple are the bas-relief carvings in the ceilings, depicting major scenes from the great Hindu epics, the

Ramayana and *Mahabharata*. The images of the ten incarnations of Lord Vishnu are carved on the walls of the shrine. The Krishna Mandir of Patan Durbar Square is undoubtedly one of the finest stone structures in the Kathmandu Valley and is thus of considerable national importance. In 1988–89 the Nepal Heritage Society and the Department of Archaeology took the initiative to its conservation. As is often the case with stone structures, it looked good from outside, but in fact the temple had been badly damaged by rainwater penetration and subsequent salt action and rusting of fixing cramps. Considerable damage was also found in the stone carvings on the cornices and friezes. At the request of Nepal Heritage Society, the Indian National Trust for Art and Cultural Heritage (INTACH) of New Delhi sent an expert to help in consolidating this massive stone structure. Thorough examination revealed that there was no danger to the structure as such, and the chemists and other technical staff of the DOA managed to complete this conservation project in the course of one year. First, waterproofing material was laid on all terraces of the temple. Then the stone blocks joined together by lime mortar were strengthened by grouting and applying new lime mortar. Effects of salts were chemically removed, and bio-deterioration of stone was controlled by applying algaecides. The pigeon droppings were cleaned, and so on.

The Char Narayan Mandir is the oldest temple in Durbar Square, constructed in NS 686 (AD 1565) by King Purandhar Singh. It stands in front of the Kartik Dabali or the open platform where the famous Kartik dance is performed every year. Next to it is the brick and stucco temple of Narasingha built in the shikhara style in 1590 by King Purandhar Singh.

The Bishwa Nath Mandir was built by King Sri Niwas Malla in 1626. This double-storey brick temple is constructed on a square base of two-tiered plinth of brick and stone. The roofs are supported by decorative struts. The carvings and decorations of this temple represent contemporary art and architecture of the 17th-century Malla period. The temple was repaired in 1956 and major restoration work was done in 1974. But on 6 August 1989, the four sides of the top roof collapsed, causing the eastern and southern roofs of the first floor to fall. The remaining northern and western side roofs were also damaged and tilted dangerously. Poor repairs carried out in 1974 and increasing vehicular traffic in the main street in front of the temple seemed to be the causes. As this was one of the most important enlisted monuments, the Nepal government immediately set about having it restored, with financial help from UNESCO's Emergency Fund. Because of difficulties in finding timbers in the Valley, however, renovation was delayed for some time. During renovation about 90% of the timber rafters on the top floor and 70% on the first floor were found unusable. All decorative wooden pieces, timber rafters, planks, face boards, carved pillars, *jhingati* tiles, clay used for mortar etc., were cleaned and chemically treated before re-use. Any missing or unrepairable carved pillars, struts, brackets and the tympanum were newly carved and used. Broken struts were joined by iron plates and knot-bolted from the back, which cannot be seen from outside, and re-used. A total of 130 new metal wind-bells *(fayagna)* were cast and fixed on both roofs. Damages to one of the two guardian elephants and both the riders on the elephant were also repaired. (Shrestha, 1992)

Another important temple in Durbar Square is Bhimsen Mandir, a large rectangular three-storey edifice. It was renovated, beautified and enlarged in 1681 by King Sri Niwas Malla. Every year a grand festival takes place on the ninth day of the dark fortnight of the month Srawan (July/August), when a small replica of Bhimsen is carried on a chariot around the city. In 1989/90 and in 1991/92, the DOA did some repair works in the main temple.

The *Manimandapa* or the Jewel Pavilion of Patan, also known as *Shorah Khutey Pati* or the 16-pillar rest house, stands in front of the famous Krishna Mandir. It is one of the two rest houses which flank the stairs leading into the ancient fountain, *Manidhara or Manga Hiti*. Adjacent to the Malla royal palace, *Manimandapa* served as the council hall and occasional coronation place of kings. *Manimandapa* was also, as it remains today, the site where priests and astrologers convene to determine the auspicious moment for initiating the annual festival of the Valley's beloved patron, the Red Machindranath. The exact foundation date of these twin Mandapas is unknown, but Manimandapa predates AD 1701, when 'the conference room of kings had become old and King Yoganarendra had it renovated'. (Tewari, 1952; Slusser and Vajracarya, 1974)

A large bell is hung on a stone structure between two stone pillars and has a metal roof with *gajuras* or pinnacles. It was built in 1736 by King Vishnu Malla and Queen Chandra Laxmi Devi and used for ceremonial purposes.

Next to the octagonal shikara-style Krishna Temple (also known as Chasilin Dewal, for the daughter of King Yog Narendra Malla, Princess Yogmati Devi) is a stone pillar erected by King Yog Narendra Malla with two statues on the top: one of his son and the other of himself, with a bird's figure perched on his head. He is said to have confided to his ministers that one would know of his death when the bird came to life and took flight. Yet another important temple of this palace square is the Hari–Shankar temple, probably constructed at about the same time as the Bishwa Nath temple was built, in 1626.

Outside the Patan Durbar Square there are numerous other important WHS monuments. The Maha Baudha temple was constructed in beginning of the 17th-century. This large terracotta edifice is located in a narrow, irregular courtyard. Unique in the Valley in terms of style and material, the whole façade is covered with terracotta plaques depicting the Lord Buddha – perhaps some nine thousand Buddha images in all. After visiting the Mahaboddhi temple of Bodh Gaya in India, a rich merchant and artist named Avayaraj decided to build a replica in Patan. The foundations were laid in 1565, and the temple was consecrated in 1601 in the presence of King Siva Singh Malla. It has sustained many natural calamities since then, but only the earthquake of 1934 did severe damage. With a donation of Nepalese rupees 3,100, the members of the temple trust and the scion of the donor Avaya Raj began to renovate it already the next year, finishing in 1938. The present shape is the result of this renovation. (Sakya, 1988)

A famous gem of Patan is the Kwa Baha, also known as Hiranya Varna Mahavihara, or the golden temple, built in the early 15th century. Legend ascribes its origins to King Bhaskar Varma of the 12th century and Pingala, a queen from Marwar in India. It stands as one of the oldest and most revered Buddhist temples of Patan.

An inscription near Kumbheshwar Temple from the AD 767, i.e. the reign of King Rudradev, mentions the inauguration of a stone waterspout, indicating that it was an important religious site already then. The grand Kumbheshwar Temple was built by a local merchant named Jayabhima in AD 1392 during the reign of King Jayasthiti Malla in memory of his deceased wife Anantalaxmi. In AD 1414, the stone waterspout known as *Misahiti* was renovated by Jasaraj Juju in memory of his deceased wife Jayalaxmi during the reign of King Jaya Kriti Malla. King Sri Niwas Malla beautified this temple, enlarging it from three to five storeys. In 1808, a big earthquake destroyed this temple completely, but a resident of Dhaugal Tole, Hanumanta Singh Amatya, renovated or reconstructed it completely in the following year. Three years later, Hanumanta Singh Amatya and his brothers repaired the pond of Kumbheshwar. The mouth of the stone waterspout was gilded and an image of Uma Maheshwar was established. Sadly, the gilded mouth was stolen in 1953.

Kumbheshwar Mahadev Mandir is the oldest existing temple in Patan. It was built in the last quarter of the 14th century AD. This is a very popular religious site, with the famous Bagla Mukhi temple in its vicinity. During *Janai Purnima*, which falls on the day of the July/August full moon, a gala festival takes place here. King Yog Narendra Malla had this temple renovated in 1697, and then in 1923 Prime Minister Bhim Shumsher Rana restored the dilapidated temple and made the area more presentable. However, the 1934 earthquake destroyed the temple completely, and its present shape is a result of the renovations carried out under Prime Minister Juddha Shumsher Rana. In 1958, King Mahendra had the waterspout, pond and periphery wall restored, and two years later, the pond known as Gosain Kunda or Gauri Kunda was repaired by the District Office. (Sakya, 1961)

Machindranath is worshipped by all as the god of rain and prosperity. The temple of Machindranath was probably built during the 17th century. The greatest festival of Patan occurs when this god is brought out on a chariot in the month of Baisakh (April/May); the celebrations later end in Jawalakhel (southern Patan) with the exhibition of a legendary ornamental vest on the day of *Bhoto Dekhaune Jatra*.

The incident of Kot Ghar or Tahaphaley of Patan Durbar was one of the most interesting episodes during my tenure of office. In March 1982 the municipal authorities started demolishing the roofs of the Kot Ghar, intending to build new offices there. This historical rest house has always been part of the palace. King Sri Niwas Malla had built it in 1678 as barracks for his personal guard. It is known as Taha Phaley, which means 'the long rest house or pati with 32 columns' (*kawals*). During the Rana era it was turned into merchandise shops; a statue of the god Bhimsen was also established there. To return to the events of March 1982: On the first day of its demolition the local people as well as the Patan Durbar Maintenance Office requested the DOA to halt this unauthorized destruction of such an important historical structure. The Lalitpur District Office also requested the Municipality to halt the demolition work. The DOA immediately took action and got the demolition stopped. Then the Municipality put pressure on the Ministry of Education and Culture for permission to demolish this structure and allow a new building to be constructed. The Ministry immediately sought the help of UNESCO, requesting their advice. The DOA also requested the District Revenue Office not to provide a land ownership certificate to the Municipality, because the site was a part of the Patan Palace. The DOA also requested the Home Ministry and the Valley Zonal Commissioner Office to take the actions necessary to halt the demolition. In the meantime UNESCO condemned the demolition of this structure and plans for the new construction – indeed, UNESCO even warned the Nepal government that such demolition and new construction might serve as a reason for de-listing Patan Durbar as a World Heritage Site. This action on the part of Patan Municipality was totally in contravention of the Ancient Monument Preservation Act as well as the World Heritage Convention. The municipal authorities kept trying to win over public opinion, but the intellectual community and the press remained vehemently critical (see e.g. Joshi, 1983). The Lalitpur District Panchayat also ruled that the decision to demolish the historical Kot Pati and construct local government offices in its place should be withdrawn (reported in *Rising Nepal,* 30 April 1983). Next, the government took possession of the Kot Pati and handed over it to Lalitpur Durbar Maintenance Office for upkeep (*Rising Nepal,* 20 July 1984). And thereby the attempt of Patan municipal authorities was foiled.

Another interesting incident concerned the Lalitpur Chamber of Commerce (LCC), in 1988. The LCC sent to the DOA drawings of its planned new building, which they wanted to construct after demolishing an old house and Saraswati Pati, situated in front of the famous Bhimsen Temple at Mangal Bazar. The DOA found that the drawings submitted for approval were not in keeping with the norms prescribed for the Patan Protected Monument Zone (PMZ), so permission was refused. The LCC followed up by trying to convince the DOA and also put political pressure to bear on the DOA, but the latter did not heed any of this. Ultimately the LCC asked the DOA for help in improving and altering the drawings. The DOA agreed to do this, and the LCC was asked to sign a bond by which the LCC pledged to retain the Saraswati Temple as before and also re-use all old wooden artefacts after proper cleaning and chemical treatment. The Saraswati Pati was indeed renovated in its original shape. The old structure was renovated and all original windows, doors, struts and other artefacts were re-used. While this building was under renovation the DOA had to intervene on numerous occasions to ensure protection of its traditional design, such as non-plastered brick walls and two-sided *jingiti* roofing. When the work was completed, it was concluded that an attempt had in fact been made to maintain some urban morphology of that area.

Next was the case of the house of Prakash Man Shrestha at Mangal Bazar. In 1987, Mr. Shrestha first demolished an old house to the north of *Manga Hiti* and adjacent to the famous Mani Kumar Ganesh Temple, and then began to construct a new modern concrete structure, without proper approval from the DOA. Upon request, the Patan municipal authorities sent the plans for the house to the DOA for approval. The DOA thoroughly studied the submitted design, and, having made some corrections and additions, then returned the plans with the necessary stamp of approval. As this house was adjacent to the Ganesh Temple, the roof height was required to be maximum one foot below the pinnacle of the temple. The owner was asked to fix doors and windows of certain standard sizes and not to put iron shutters on the ground floor. Instead, he built the house ignoring all the norms and conditions put forth by the DOA. The DOA then immediately halted the construction work with the help of the CDO. This building remained unfinished for several years, but work was taken up again during fluid political situation of Jana Andolan I in 1989/90.

A more positive note can be added: during the Third SAARC Summit in 1987, the DOA with the help of local authorities was able to stop numerous illegal constructions in Patan monument zone.

In Durbar Square some monuments were restored with the help of UNESCO/WHC and the Kathmandu Valley Preservation Trust (KVPT). In 1992 the KVPT completed the restoration of Radha Krishna Temple inside the Patan Monument Zone, with financial assistance from the Canadian Overseas Development Fund. The complete refurbishment of this outstanding example of a Malla period temple has been praised by numerous experts, including the 1993 UNESCO Mission to Nepal, who termed it 'a demonstration that the highest standards of international conservation practice have been achieved in Nepal'. In the same year the 16th century Uma Maheheswar temple situated at Kwaalku Tole was restored, thanks to funding from the British Ambassador's Small Grant Fund. The KVPT has undertaken many other lesser repair and conservation projects inside the Patan Durbar Protected Monument Zone, such as roof repairs to Mani Gufa, Kwalkhu Pati restoration, Lakhe Shrestha Tower restoration and Patukva Agam Chhen restoration from 1992 to 1997. In 2006 KVPT restored the 17th-century Laxmi Narayan Temple of the Patan Durbar World Heritage Site.

German assistance has also been received in developing and maintaining several infrastructures, including stone spouts in the PMZ of Patan. In the Zone many national and international donor agencies have been actively participating in heritage conservation. In 1990/91 the UNESCO–Japan Funds-in-Trust Project spent about USD 376,000 simply on preparing drawings, photographs and a conservation programme for Sundari Chowk – in fact, a sum that could have sufficed to complete the restoration and rehabilitation of this palace courtyard as a whole.

Unlike in other Durbar Squares of the Valley, local traditional houses surround the Patan Durbar Square. Until recently, this was also the only commercial centre of the city. As a result during times of political turmoil, many old and traditional houses on both sides of the streets leading into Patan Durbar Square have been demolished and new concrete buildings constructed, defacing the whole morphology of the area.

In Patan Monument Zone several unique restoration projects have been completed, among them the reconstruction of the dilapidated pilgrim rest house Ayu Guthi Sattal, north of Manga Hiti and next to the Mani Ganesh temple in the vicinity of the Patan Durbar is worth mentioning. This building, of prime importance forming the northern edge of the WHS of Patan Durbar Square, was probably constructed in 1703 and then rebuilt after the earthquake of 1934. *Sattals* or rest houses in the Newa cities of the Kathmandu Valley take many forms. One can distinguish a *sattal* from a *pati* by its provision of a closed room of sorts, usually on an upper floor, where one can stay. Both *sattals* and *patis* may include shrines.

The only religio-cultural event takes place here is the annual *puja* (worship) at Pausa Purnima. A document from AD 1852 describes the *puja* at Pausa Purnima at Ayu Guthi: 12 *Yomaris* (sweet pastries), one duck, one goat and *Kagha* player during the *puja*. A Mandala should be drawn inside the house on the first floor, as for *Bhaitika*. Hot water should be given to the *guthiars* to wash their hands, legs and mouth. *Tashi* fruit should be worshipped and a duck sacrificed at the nearby Bhimsen temple.

In November 1994 the DOA gave approval to the KVPT to under take the Ayu Guthi Sattal Restoration Project. Then the ownership problem emerged. As legal procedure in Nepal takes a long time, the DOA took the advice of the Ministry of Law to find a quicker solution and immediately start restoration before the *sattal* collapsed totally. In February 1995 the Ministry of Law recommended that the building be nationalized under section 7 of the AMPA, in light of the owner's inability to maintain a monument of artistic and historical importance – the first case of nationalizing a monument in Nepal due to its endangered status. In March 1996 the Nepal government paid generous compensation to the caretaker of this *sattal* and decided to nationalize it. An extended battle from 1996 to 1999 upheld the government's move to nationalize the dilapidated structure. But against this decision the caretaker filed a case in the Supreme Court. The legal battle to secure this historic building was won in a landmark victory for Nepal – but not until 24 March 1999. By this time the *sattal* had indeed collapsed and the actual historic building was lost.

Once the building had fallen down, the only alternative was to reconstruct it to a condition similar to that of 1991. The Ayu Guthi Sattal reconstruction project was started in January 2001; by July 2002 it was completed. But some confusion was created by the decision to reconstruct. Questions were raised whether it was worthwhile or appropriate to reconstruct a building that had lost almost all its original historical fabric. However, also this building was in fact a many-layered palimpsest. After the earthquakes, it had been rebuilt with many borrowed elements, and stood as a very bad example of earlier restoration attempts. Moreover, at a time when the Kathmandu Valley was facing ongoing losses of historic buildings in its WHS and after fighting a long battle to save this building, the DOA and KVPT became morally responsible for reconstructing it. Thus the size, plinth height, wall thickness, structural roof and floor framing, roof cover, and overall form of the building were replicated.

The rich historical patina of the façade has now been reconstructed. All the timber and woodwork has been completely replaced and the lost plinth has also been reconstructed. Wherever possible, all art works have been replaced *in situ.* Taking into consideration the frequent seismic threats in Nepal, the structure has been strengthened by using concealed stainless steel bolting on rafters; concealed iron angles coated with anti-corrosive paint have been used for connecting wall plates; and the wall of the front façade has been reinforced with stainless steel wire. Copper sheets provide damp-proofing of the ground floor, and plasti-felt has been used as waterproof membranes beneath the traditional mud bed on which the tiles rest. All timbers, rafters and woodworks have been chemically treated against termite attack, and a herbicide, karmex, has been used to control plant growth on the roof. Old tiles *(jhingati)* have been laid after soaking them in siltrete solution for roofing (Theophile &Ranjitkar, 1999; Kathmandu Valley Preservation Trust, 2002).

Patukva Agam Chhen Restoration Project, one of the earlier restoration efforts of the KVPT, gave back to the city of Patan and the world a rare architectural treasure. This is one of a handful of esoteric shrine buildings used by the royal priests, an architectural monument of international stature. The building remains in the hands of the priestly family, which first built this structure. Thus in its restored state it can be used again for religious rituals of this priestly clan resident in the adjacent courtyards.

The building was in ruins in 1992 when the project was identified. Restoration work began in winter 1993 and was completed in late March 1997. Conceptually, the project set an important precedent in preservation in Nepal, for a several reasons. First, owned by a religious *guthi* confraternity, it was one of the first semi-private monuments to be restored with international assistance in Patan. Until now international attention had concentrated on government-owned or public buildings, ignoring the hundreds of threatened A-class monuments under semi-private (*guthi* or *sangha*) or private ownership. For this special case, the project developed a model tripartite agreement between the owners, the KVPT and the DOA, a framework which both protected it in the future and allowed turn-key implementation by the KVPT. Contributions and agreement stipulations also included a substantial local contribution of approximately $5,000. Despite the delays in collecting this local contribution, the importance of financial participation of local partners cannot be underestimated – it is critical to the long-term future of Nepal's heritage and as a guarantee of ongoing local commitment to maintain the building.

A second point: At the time of project inception, the actual shrine stood outside the delineated WHS. The rallying of funds for a structure which defined but stood outside the boundary line – i.e. technically an unlisted monument – was an important precedent for international attention to historical buildings which are vital to the national heritage but have remained unprotected.

Thirdly, the seismic strengthening of this monument introduced a new approach to protecting the fragile masonry structures of Nepalese architecture. Instead of rebuilding the walls, the existing masonry structures were left untouched wherever possible and a new reinforcing 'back-up frame' somewhat like interior scaffolding was introduced in the interior. Previously, all seismic strengthening measures in Nepal had introduced concrete ring beams into the existing wall fabric.

During restoration it was found that after the 1934 earthquake the building had been replicated in line with its earlier condition. The project succeeded in maintaining some of the historical fabric of this building. Seismic strengthening elements such as timber back-up frame was also provided. The timber back-up frame may prove to have wide scope for application in Nepal because it is easy to build and effective for reinforcing smaller structures against earthquakes. Similar to the visible steel frame of the German-funded Cyasilin Mandap Reconstruction Project, this is the only contemporary example of a secondary structural frame in timber added to buttress a building. This approach to reinforcement, the back-up frame, reduces the need for invasive insertion of structure in the walls. It would be less costly and appropriate for larger buildings if executed in steel. I believe this may be a major positive direction for earthquake strengthening technology in Nepal. The use of a timber back-up frame on the interior to strengthen the fragile tower-like building against earthquakes has been described as a useful model by Sir Bernard Feilden, who reviewed the project design in 1994. (See Theophile & Ranjitkar, 1998) The completion of the Patukva Agam Chhen restoration project has been hailed as a success by UNESCO experts as well. (See *i.a.* Theophile & Ranjitkar, 1999.)

Lakhe Shrestha Agam, a 17th-century shrine house, was an emergency restoration project launched by the KVPT in the Patan Monument Zone in November 1995. The Lakhe Shrestha Agam well demonstrates the beauty of Malla period architecture and the craft of Newa carpenters. Its fine courtyard façade and impressive rooftop tower are key examples of Patan's artistic legacy. This tower, called *phuja* in Newari, defines one edge of Patan's Durbar Square, one of the greatest collections of historic towers on earth.

In the course of the project, the pinnacle *(gajura)* was restored and properly cleaned before reinstallation. Historical rafters were repaired and lost rafters replaced with new ones, as were all eaves boards. Where possible, the historical timber apron and panelling was repaired and lost members were provided, matching historical design. All damaged *pakha dali* in historical timber was replaced.

From 1978 to 1996 the Nippon Institute of Technology (NIT) of Japan and the DOA worked together and prepared reports on the architecture of ancient palaces and Buddhist monasteries after making a photographic survey. The results were published in two volumes. (See Nippon Institute of Technology, Research Mission, 1981 & 1985.)

Between 1990 and 1996, the NIT also helped Nepal in restoring and rehabilitating one of Patan's oldest Buddhist monasteries – I-Baha Bahi, an excellent example of recent conservation activities. The monastery was built in AD 1427 and according to available records was restored in 1661. This building, designed according to accurate measurement systems, exhibits the sophisticated and solid architectural style of the *bahis* of the Malla period. It had suffered considerable damage in the earthquake of 1681 and was probably rebuilt or renovated in 1710. It seems that after a series of earthquakes in the Kathmandu Valley in 1767, 1808 and 1833, the *bahi* was renovated in 1880. After that it was left uncared for nearly more than a century, until 1990, when a joint Nepal-Japan team began renovation work. After the dismantling process was finished, the foundation of the building was strengthened by concrete slabs, which were later overlaid with bricks. Similarly, concrete was cast and base stones were set to take the pillars of the pedestal surrounding the courtyard. The project was completed in January 1996, and was handed over to Patan Municipality for proper utilization and maintenance. (For further details, see S. Manandhar, 2000.)

In 1997 with the co-operation of UDLE/GTZ and Lalitpur Sub-Metropolitan authorities, a Patan Heritage Conservation Action Plan (Master Plan) was prepared and launched. This action plan proposes several innovative ideas for protecting and regenerating the old spirit of the city core of Patan. It recommends an autonomous body to manage the conservation plan in the Patan Protected Monument Zone (PMZ). Further, it envisages steps for arresting the negative impact of modernization in the PMZ and controlling the ongoing deterioration of heritage sites, especially the traditional housing stock, which is threatened by demolition, new construction and poor adaptation. It has also tried to achieve visual as well as economic improvements for the historic centre of Patan by halting the insidious decay of the cultural environment. As means to achieve these objectives, recognition is to be given to safeguarding the intrinsic value of streetscapes, public courtyards, and other open spaces; with continuing support to the DOA in monument conservation projects, assisting house owners with the rehabilitation of their traditional houses rather than their demolition, and – importantly – working together with all stakeholders in heritage conservation. For some years, this Master Plan was implemented with the assistance of UDLE, but what is happening to it at present is not clear. (For text of the Master Plan, see Sanday Kentro Associates, 1999.)

Thanks to the efforts of some local entrepreneurs, we have in Patan several examples of successful and good conservation. These local efforts have been greatly aided by UMEPD–Asia Urbs Project, financed by the European Union. During this project period, the 'Lalitpur Heritage Award' has attracted the interest of local residents, and the restoration and rehabilitation of 'Shrestha House', 'Amatya House' and 'Tamrakar House' could become a success. At present the Patan Durbar Maintenance Office and the Heritage Unit of Patan Municipality both are trying their best to control the construction of illegal houses, but with only partial success. According to a recent report (in *Gorakhapatra* daily newspaper, 25 Chaitra, BS 2058), in Patan there are 86 houses built against the norms prescribed by the DOA and 17 houses built without any proper permits or documents. Within the Patan Durbar Monument Zone there are numerous instances of houses constructed against the prescribed building codes. Likewise, many historic buildings have been pulled down to make room for inappropriate new constructions of illegal height, both in the Durbar Square itself and in adjacent lanes and squares. During the 1990s, many traditional houses of the late 19th century, which were situated on two rows of the street going from Pulchowk to Mangal Bazar via Ga-Bahal, were mercilessly demolished. They have been replaced by modern concrete structures, damaging the beautiful cityscape of Old Patan. Within the course of only one year, from 1994 to 1995, many traditional houses were demolished inside the WHS of Patan Durbar. In spring 1994 an historic resthouse of great artistic importance was dismantled and replaced by an encroaching concrete structure. During the same time, several old houses located along the lane between Ga-Bahal and Na-Pasal, in poor condition but having important historical windows, were demolished in order to broaden the passage for vehicular traffic. At Kwalkhu, two 19th-century residences of artistic and urban-cultural importance were demolished in March 1995.

In 2006 the World Monuments Watch included the Patan Palace complex in its 2005 list of the world's most important and threatened monuments in need of emergency intervention. Then in May 2006, a joint mission consisting of the KVPT and the UNESCO World Heritage Centre, in collaboration with the DOA, drafted a report for the conservation and development of Patan Palace complex. This has become known as the Patan Royal Palace Restoration Project. Fund-raising programmes have already been launched – which is very encouraging – and donations are pouring in from various international agencies.

Every year the DOA carries out repair and maintenance work in the Patan Durbar Monument Zone. In this connection, mention should also be made of the successful three-year renovation of the Court Building in the south of Sundari Chowk. On the other hand, it should not be forgotten that Patan still has numerous monuments and private buildings awaiting renovation and proper care.

Krishna Mandir before the earthquake of 1934

Monuments around Patan Durbar Square before the earthquake of 1934

Patan Durbar Square from the south, early 1920s. (Courtesy: Images of Nepal, page 92).

Restoration of Degu Talle Temple and other monuments of Patan Durbar Square in 2003.

Patan Durbar square from the south (Courtesy: Clarence C. Taylor, ca. 1863, Royal Geographical Society, S 0003074) Also published in the Patan Royal Palace Restoration Project, Joint Mission Report, December 2006.

View of Patan Durbar Square from the southwest, (Courtesy: Kurt Boeck, 1899, Museum für Volkerkunde, Vienna, also published in the Patan Royal Palace Restoration Project, Joint Mission Report, December 2006, p.8)

Historic view of Bhashmeshvara Mandir, Sundari Chowk, Patan Durbar and the southwest corner of the Court Building. (Courtesy: Kurt Boeck, 1899, Museum fur Volkerkunde, Vienna, also published in the Patan Royal Palace Restoration Project, Joint Mission report, December, 2006.p.66) The temple was totally destroyed in the earthquake of 1934.

Main façade of Keshav Narayan Chowk of Patan Durbar and Degu Talle Temple before the earthquake of 1934. (Personal collection)

Main façade of Keshav Narayan Chowk of Patan Durbar and Degu Talle Temple after renovation in 1980

Principal façade of Mul Chowk, Patan Durbar (Courtesy: Perceval Landon, 1922)

Earthquake of 1934: The roof and bell tower pavilion severely damaged and the Degu Talle Temple behind has collapsed completely. (Personal collection)

Destruction caused by the earthquake of 1934 to Patan Durbar Square around the Taleju Bell. (Courtesy: Images of Nepal, page 95)

Mahabodha Temple, Patan

Director-General of UNESCO Mr. Rene Maheu at Keshav Narayan Chowk, Patan Durbar, in 1972.

Early 20th c. photograph of the Court Building, Patan (Published in the Patan Royal Palace Restoration Project, Joint Mission Report, December 2006, p. 70)

Kot-pati around 1900 (Published in the Patan Royal Palace Restoration Project, Joint Mission Report, December 2006, p. 68)

Keshav Narayan Chowk of Patan Durbar after restoration in 2000

Sundari Chowk and Tusha Hiti of Patan Durbar, 1975

Mul Chowk of Patan Durbar, 1975

A private house within Patan Monument Zone, reconstructed with carved windows with dachi appa façade (Recent photo).

5

Conservation of Bhaktapur Durbar Monument Zone

Bhaktapur, 'the city of devotees', is the third of the major cities of the Kathmandu Valley. It lies about 16 kilometres east of Kathmandu, and has a population of about one hundred thousand. Bhaktapur is a city of unusual cultural and religious richness, with a very complex society, predominantly Hindu. The majority of its people are farmers, who also produce household goods like clay pots, straw mattresses, cloth and the famous *juju dhau,* or 'royal curd'. Though Bhaktapur is not far from Kathmandu, the way of life there is quite different.

Bhaktapur is a virtual museum of arts and architecture. Each and every piece of art tells the history of the city. The monuments and sculptures reflect centuries-old techniques of craftsmanship. The city has suffered much from earthquakes, especially those of 1808, 1833 and 1934. They destroyed a considerable part of its buildings, few of which are now older than 150 years. And yet, despite the destruction, the external appearance of the city does not seem to have altered greatly. Temples have usually been preserved, if only in reduced form. Many buildings have collapsed but have been rebuilt. All these changes have not led to any substantial re-modelling: the basic structure of the town seems intact. In the late 1970s, the pioneering Bhaktapur Development Project, with financial and technical assistance from the German government, restored considerable portions of the city's lost heritage and improved its physical infrastructure.

The ancient name of Bhaktapur was *Khopring*. Over the years, this became pronounced *Khopa,* and that term is still in use in the Valley. During the Lichchavi period it was a prosperous settlement. The Thukuri monarch, King Ananda Deva, formally established the city in the 12th-century (1147–67 AD) and had the Tripura Palace constructed. This palace originally had 99 courtyards, but by the 18th century only 12 remained intact and today there is hardly half that number preserved.

In the 14th century, King Jayasthiti Malla made Bhaktapur the capital city of his kingdom. His grandson Yaksha Malla expanded the kingdom and fortified the capital in the following century. After the death of King Yaksha Malla, the city remained dormant for many generations. In 1673 AD, when Jitamitra Malla became the ruler of Bhaktapur, peace prevailed among the kingdoms of the Valley, and art and architecture began to flourish. Jitamitra Malla, Bhupatindra Malla and his son Ranjit Malla were not only three great rulers of Bhaktapur, but also three great builders, who contributed to make the city the cultural capital of Nepal.

The Durbar Square of Bhaktapur differs slightly from that of Kathmandu or Patan, where palaces and temples are united into one square complex. In Bhaktapur the main two temples, Nyatapola and Bhairabnath or Kasi Bishwanath, are situated in a square slightly lower than the dominant Durbar complex. Moreover, in contrast to Kathmandu and Patan, the old palace is not located in the centre of the city, but on its northern boundary.

The main attraction of Bhaktapur's Durbar Square is the famous Golden Gate or *Sundhoka,* built by King Ranjit Malla in 1753 AD. The British historian Perceval Landon has praised it as 'the most exquisitely designed and finished piece of gilded metalwork in all Asia'. It is highly ornate and the panels around the doorframe represent the pinnacle of artistic metalworking. The gate is capped with a small gilded roof with decorated finials. The extremely intricate *torana* or tympanum over the doorway depicts the great goddess Mahasakti, or Durga. At present this gate serves as the main entrance to the palace courtyards including Mul Chowk and Kumari Chowk – the latter was built by King Jagat Joyti Malla (early 17th-

century). Facing the Golden Gate stand two different palace wings. The one on the left was built by King Jagat Joyti Malla and now houses the National Art Gallery. The main entrance of the National Art Gallery features two lion statues, Narasimha and Hanumanta Bhairav, erected by King Bhupatindra Malla in the 18th-century.

The Malati Chowk was constructed by King Bhupatindra Malla. At present it is used as a part of the National Art Gallery. A medieval stone waterspout is an interesting attraction of this courtyard. This portion of the palace received its present appearance during the 20th century under the Ranas, when it was renovated and renamed *Lal Baithak* or 'Red Hall'.

Especially famous is the building on the right side of the Golden Gate: this is the Palace of Fifty-five Windows, built by King Yaksha Malla in AD 1420. Its present look was given by King Bhupatindra Malla. It has three storeys with finely carved doors and windows. The walls of the first floor are full of extraordinarily beautiful murals depicting scenes from the *Mahabharata,* the great Hindu epic, and of a prince going to war and hunting. The central portrait is that of the cosmic manifestation of Shiva, multi-headed, multi-armed and embracing his consort Shakti. The upper floor has the hall that features the famed 55 arcade windows. This part of the palace was severely damaged during the earthquake of 1934, but was later renovated by the Ranas.

The earthquake of August 1988 further damaged the Palace of Fifty-five Windows, most evident in the displacement of the principal façade, where in some locations the wall had become separated from interior bearing partitions by several centimetres. Unfortunately, the most serious damage was to the main rooms of the second floor, which house fine 18th century wall paintings in the Rajasthani style depicting scenes from the life of the Lord Krishna. These wall paintings have recently being restored, thanks to assistance from the Instituto per il Medio ed Estremo Oriente (ISMEO), Rome.

The first concern of any restoration project will be to consolidate the bearing structure, so as to prevent further damage. On the basis of the preliminary proposal for restoration submitted by the author, who was then Acting Director-General of the DOA, and the Conservation Project Proposal prepared by Niels Gutschow and Gotz Hagmuller together with Professor Walter Mann and others in April

1993, a tripartite agreement was signed between Nepal's Ministry of Education, Culture and Social Welfare, the Federal Republic of Germany, and companies of the Soaltee Group to preserve the historic Palace of Fifty-five Windows and its wall paintings, on 30 September 1994. Unfortunately, inner politicking prevented the project from materializing in time, and ultimately both the German government and the Soaltee Group withdrew. Then Bhaktapur Municipality and the DOA turned to UNESCO. With the help of UNESCO, a national workshop on the conservation of the palace was organized in Bhaktapur in March 2000, with the participation of all stakeholders. Still, actual restoration activities could start only after a delay of more than four years. In April 2004, an agreement for the restoration of the Palace of Fifty-five Windows was signed between the Department of Archaeology and Bhaktapur Municipality. Total costs were estimated to approximately RS 160,000,000. In October 2003 it was decided to finish this project within three years, but, some four years later, it is not yet complete, and the estimated costs have also risen to some two hundred million rupees. Although the experts have said that they are confident they can renovate the palace using traditional methods, exactly what has delayed the completion of this project no one can say – nor are the final results certain. How they will conserve the ancient murals and the fragile walls holding them, and how they will be strengthen the whole building from earthquake shock, remain to be seen?

Jamdar Chowk, with a Tantric Shiva Linga in the centre, is the first courtyard immediately after the Golden Gate. After Jamdar Chowk comes Beko Chowk or 'zig-zag' courtyard. A large stone slab is kept here, a symbol of Kestrapal, the god of the area or fields. From Beko Chowk we reach Mul Chowk, at the entrance to which an armed guard is posted round the clock. Only Nepalis are allowed to enter this courtyard. The Mul Chowk is the oldest structure in the palace complex, richly decorated by generations of kings of Bhaktapur. The temple of the royal patron goddess Tulaja or Taleju stands here. Available records say the courtyard has been in existence since at least the 14th century. King Naresh Malla did some renovation work on the Taleju Temple and added a few sandalwood windows in Mul Chowk in 1637. In NS 826 (AD 1706) King Bhupatindra Malla renovated the temple of the goddess Taleju, repairing the roof and the gilded eleven pinnacles. He erected the statue of a lion to the right and a *betal* to the left of the pinnacles. He also renovated the palace wing of Mul Chowk, fixed it with windows made of various types of fine wood and decorated it with beautiful mural paintings.

Bhairav Chowk, to the south of Mul Chowk, was constructed during the 16th century. King of Kathmandu Sadha Siva Malla was once kept in confinement in this courtyard because of his sexual perversions. Since then this courtyard has been known as the Sadha Siva Chowk. Another of its names is 'Dafoo-Swan Chowk'. A sculpture of Varahi, the consort of Varaha, the wild boar incarnation of Vishnu, is installed here; thus it is also known as Varahi Chowk. This courtyard is full of beautiful woodcarvings.

King Jitamitra Malla began renovating the Kumari Chowk in 1677; this work took him fifteen years to complete. He also renovated Hiti Chowk and Nag Pokhari. An inscription dated NS 808 (AD 1688/89) states that this monarch built the royal palace *Thanathunim* with *Lu-Hiti* or gilded waterspout, gardens, courtyards and the pond or Nag Pokhari with a beautiful gilded *nag* hood or canopy, and a sunken royal bathing pool situated in the northeastern corner .

Jitamitra Malla also renovated Bhairav Chowk and Sadha Siva Chowk, most probably in NS 837 (AD 1717). In 1990, a joint team of the DOA and the Guthi Undertaking renovated Kumari Chowk, but other important courtyards still await renovation, among them Mul Chowk and Sadha Siva Chowk. The old Basantapur Durbar was renovated by King Bhupatindra Malla and also by his son King Ranajit Malla. But this palace was completely destroyed in the earthquake of 1934. The Ranas did not renovate it: it was demolished and turned into a garden, where at present the premises of Shree Padma High School stand (built in 1946).

As almost all important courtyards of this palace are closed to outsiders, the visitor has to be satisfied with the diversity of monuments around the palace complex. Entering Bhaktapur gate, on the right one notes two temples. One is the two-tiered Krishna Temple, with roof struts depicting the ten incarnations of Vishnu. The second is a terracotta shikhara temple dedicated to the Goddess Durga, or Bhagawati.

The life-sized statue of King Bhupatindra Malla atop a pillar is another remarkable piece of art. The last Malla ruler of Bhaktapur, King Ranjit Malla erected this statue in 1753 as a tribute to his father Bhupatindra Malla, who was responsible for enriching the cultural heritage of Bhaktapur beyond comparison.

The big bell, installed here by King Ranjit Malla in 1737, is used while worshipping the goddess Tulaja Bhawani. Behind this statue there is a beautiful stone shikara-style temple of the goddess Batsala, built in 1672 by King Jagat Prakash Malla, with nine pinnacles. King Bhupatindra Malla renovated this temple in 1700. The main interesting feature of this temple is its gilded finial and wind-bells – very unusual on shikhara-style temples. The bell on the lower plinth of the temple was placed there by King Bhupatindra Malla, to counteract the ominous tone of the death knell he had heard in a dream.

Next to the Batsala Temple is another temple in almost the same style, dedicated to the goddess Bhagawati. On the relief panel series in front of the sanctum, various forms of *matrikas* or mother goddesses are depicted.

King Yaksha Malla built Yaksheshvara Mahadev Temple, also known as Pashupatinath Temple, in the 15th century. It was reconstructed by King Jitamitra Malla in 1692 and again rebuilt after the great earthquake of 1934. The supporting roof struts depict various forms of Shiva and his family. The sanctum has the four-faced Shiva Linga, and the god is worshipped every morning and evening. In 1999 Bhaktapur Municipality repaired it with funds generated from tourist entry fees.

Taumadhi Square, one of the three main squares of Bhaktapur, is located in the centre of the city. This square is dominated by two of Bhaktapur's grandest temples. The Nyatapvala or five-storey temple of the goddess Siddhi Laxmi, the personal deity of King Bhupatindra Malla, is the most majestic. Its five-step base gives it a towering height which makes it the tallest temple in the kingdom. The temple stairway is lined with pairs of stone figures. At the bottom stand two legendary wrestlers, Jaimal and Patta, as *duarapalas* or guards. It is believed that they possess the strength of ten ordinary people. Then come figures of elephants, lions, *sharduls*, *sinhini* and *byaghrini* placed according to their increasing power. This grand temple, a masterpiece of Nepalese architecture, was built by King Bhupatindra Malla in 1702 AD. The columns around the temple sanctum and doorframe are beautifully carved. The impressive woodwork includes 108 supporting roof struts, which depict the diverse forms of the goddess Bhagawati, or Mahismardini, and other associate deities. History maintains that while building this temple King Bhupatindra himself carried bricks to the site to inspire his people, who then carried sufficient materials in five days to complete the work. In the earthquake of 1934 only the topmost roof of this grand temple fell down, and later on it was repaired. In 1962 some repair works were undertaken, and in 1998–99 Bhaktapur Municipality rebuilt the roof with revenues generated from tourism. The Nyatapvala Temple is one of two five-tiered pagodas surviving in the Kathmandu Valley, a royal donation of exquisite proportions and silhouette. (For further details of the construction and consecration of the temple see Vaidya, 2004.)

In the southeast corner of this courtyard there stands a massive three-storey rectangular temple to Bhairav, also known as Kashi Bishwanath. The original temple is believed to have been constructed in NS 121 (AD 1001) during the reign of King Nirvaya Deva. When King Ananda Deva (1145–65) built Bhaktapur, he made it an axis point of the city. Later Malla rulers reconstructed the temple. King Bhupatindra Malla gave it its present shape with three roofs and seven storeys.

King Bishwa Malla renovated the small temple of the god Bhairav and established an image of the deity. It was later renovated, extended, and enlarged by King Bhupatindra Malla in NS 838 (AD 1718), after the completion of Nyatapvala Temple. This temple was totally destroyed in the earthquake of 1934 but was reconstructed in 1941 by members of the Mathema family. Some decades later, Bhaktapur Municipality took full responsibility for its restoration, in a project that commenced in Magsir 2052 BS (November 1995) and was completed in September 1996 – in less than one year's time. Unfortunately, although this recent restoration seemed to be adequate from the outside, it neither improved the inner structures and floors nor provided necessary facilities for pilgrims. This time Mr. Daya Ram Bhakta Mathema of the Mathema family repaired and re-fabricated the gilded *pasuka Jhhal* or small-carved windows of the second floor, at a cost of 400,000 rupees.

Further south there is an adjoining temple courtyard, the Narayan Chowk. In it is located a two-storey temple of Tilmadhav (also called the Narayan Temple), dedicated to the Lord Vishnu. This temple was constructed during the 11th century but its present appearance dates from the 18th century. In front of the entrance are three pillars featuring attributes of Vishnu, with his riding-mount Garuda in the centre, surrounded by his discus and conch.

The Tacapal or Dattatraya Square is one of the three main squares of Bhaktapur. The Dattatraya temple stands in the east of the square. It was built by King Yaksha Malla (AD 1428–82) and his son Bishwa Malla, the ruler of Bhaktapur (1548–60) and Queen Gangarani in 1589. Originally built as a *mandapa* or open assembly hall, it was later enlarged by Yaksha Malla as a pilgrims' rest house and then expanded to form the temple as it stands today, serving both as a rest house and as an important shrine. The god Dattatraya represents the Hindu trinity of the Lords Brahma, Vishnu and Maheshwar (or Shiva). In front of the temple, statues of two wrestlers stand as guards. There are three columns with Garuda, discus and conch – the vehicle (mount) and weapons of Vishnu. The original building was a *sattal* of square *mandapa* plan very similar to Kasthamandapa, and was also known as *Tao Capala* or 'the grand rest house'. The surrounding locality is still known as Tacapal. Some historians believe that the eldest son of Yaksha Malla, Raya Malla, added one floor to this structure (Munakarmi, 1984, p. 143). Possibly it was turned into a temple during the reign of King Bishwa Malla, who added a further floor, making it a three-storey structure. Extensive changes were made to the existing structure and a new element, a small ancillary porch, was joined to the western façade of the old building. It seems that it was again renovated by King Jitamitra Malla (1673–96), but, according to the Garuda pillar or *stambha* inscription, the curious porch that has so radically compromised the original building was not added until 1849. It, together with the gilt doorway of the sanctum, was donated by the presiding *mahanta* or priest in memory of his guru's guru. (Slusser & Vajracarya, 1974)

Surrounding the Dattatraya Square are several *maths* or monasteries, of which the most important is Pujari Math. Located to the southeast behind the Dattatraya Temple, it was built in the 15th-

century. This makes it the oldest existing Hindu monastery in the Valley, although it was extended and altered by a *mahanta* (priest) in the 18th-century. It also suffered considerable damage during the 1934 earthquake. The Pujari Math is especially known for the rich, finely nuanced 18th century woodcarvings that grace its doors and windows. Particularly beautiful is the famed 'Peacock Window', which faces the lane on the east side of the building. It depicts a majestic peacock in the centre, with outspread wings serving as a lattice pattern for the circular opening of the window.

The Pujari Math was built as a residence-cum-office for the priest of the famous Dattatraya Temple, most probably during the reign of King Yaksha Malla (AD 1428–82). It was reconstructed during the reign of King Bishwa Malla (1548–60) after being severely damaged by an earthquake. Tradition says that extensive repair work was undertaken when Kripala Giri and Loknath Giri were the priests-in-charge. Inscriptions dated AD 1763 situated in the middle courtyard of the Math also say it was renovated in the 18th century as well. Thus, in every century a thoroughgoing renovation of the existing structure has been undertaken. In fact the present architecture of the Math largely stems from the last king of Bhaktapur, Ranjit Malla, and the edifice as it stands today is vastly different from 15th-century original. Evidence indicates that many wooden structures, particularly the carvings, date from the 18th century. The great earthquake of 1934 caused extensive damage to this building. It was repaired, but very badly, and for many decades it remained a ruined building. Then in 1969 the government of Germany presented a grant assistance of DM 100,000 for the renovation of Pujari Math to the Nepal government as a wedding gift to the then Crown Prince Birendra. Restoration work started in August 1971 and was completed by May 1972. This was the ever-first conservation project in which outside experts were involved, and some foreign techniques were also used. The intention was to revitalize dozens of traditional building techniques, including the production of veneer bricks of a type unique to these historical buildings. Rotted timber decorative elements were re-carved following extant examples, although figurative carvings were generally not reproduced, so as not to compete with surviving originals. (Theophile & Gutschow, 2003, p. 14). After renovation, it was transformed into a museum of Neplese woodcarving, with technical and financial assistance from the German government.

The Bhimasen Temple is a two-storey rectangular building constructed in early 17th-century. The inner sanctum features an unusual earthen image of the god Bhimasen, a puissant hero of the *Mahabbharata* and the god of power, strength and good fortunte. The gilded roof of the shrine is capped by copper pinnacles.

In the northeast of the courtyard stands Chikampha Math, which now houses the Brass and Bronze Museum. Here are displayed non-iconic bronze objects used for household tasks and various rites and rituals.

Among the three principle cities of the Kathmandu Valley, Bhaktapur offers a rare glimpse of a very nearly intact medieval city. Bhaktapur Durbar Square, Taumadhi Square and Tacapal Square were all inscribed in the UNESCO World Heritage List in 1979. Bhaktapur Monument Zone was declared as a protected monument zone in 1984, and was later extended and re-defined in 1996.

As mentioned, already in 1969 on the occasion of the wedding of the now late King Birendra, the government of Federal Republic of Germany offered a turn-key restoration project for Pujari Math, a Hindu monastery famed for its woodcarvings, as a gift to the kingdom. This was the first restoration project ever launched in Nepal with the technical and financial assistance of a foreign country, and paved the way for the inception of the Bhaktapur Development Project in 1974, which lasted for eleven years. The main objective of this project was 'to improve the living conditions of the people of Bhaktapur' through self-sustained development of the town. The people of Bhaktapur are deeply religious and tradition-bound but also heirs to an abundance of traditional skills. The restoration and preservation of buildings with high religious, cultural and architectural significance to the local people was a task which could motivate them to become involved in planning their own future. It not only provided an immense opportunity for the people to demonstrate their long-cherished but dormant traditional skills, but also gave a significant economic boost to those in the lower income brackets. This was the first conservation project in Nepal to make conservation, preservation and restoration the main task of integrated urban renewal and development possible.

The Bhaktapur Development Project (BDP) was launched in four phases. The first phase was the restoration project, which lasted for two years (1974–76). During this period, restoration was carried out on valuable monuments – public, semi-public and private – which were in a dire state of disrepair. In the second phase (1976–80), preservation and restoration remained the guiding principle of project activities, but more attention and resources were put into constructing the necessary infrastructure. During the third phase (1980–83), restoration and infrastructure work continued, but with emphasis on greater involvement of the local people. Priority was given to their demands, in line with the political situation in the country. In recognition of the need for a permanent institution for repair, maintenance and restoration of monuments, the Bhaktapur Monument Maintenance Office (MMO) was established in 1986 under the umbrella of the Department of Archaeology.

Since its establishment, the MMO has been responsible for providing regular maintenance of all monuments restored by the BDP. In addition, it has also carried out the restoration of five other monuments which had been left unfinished by the BDP in 1986. The purpose of establishing the MMO was to encourage and involve people's participation in heritage conservation. Initially, people's participation was achieved in some small projects such as restoration of the Guhyesvari Pati at Siddha Pokhari, and the Dharmakirtivihara in Kvathandu.

The BDP was completed in 1986. Its activities included considerable roof rebuilding and the introduction of ring-beams for seismic reinforcement, modeled on the practices of the UNESCO project at Hanuman Dhokha in Kathmandu. Some 30 more ambitious restorations included the dismantling and re-erection of building, sometimes using historical photographs to reproduce lost elements, were carried out during the project period. (Theophile & Gutschow, 2003, p. 15). Within a decade, the BDP successfully restored, repaired and rehabilitated about 186 buildings and monuments. It could to some extent revive the character of Bhaktapur as a historic Newa town, giving a new and fresh look to this old city. This project also enlightened and encouraged the people not only of Bhaktapur but also of other parts of the Valley and elsewhere, in preserving their cultural heritage – especially the built heritage. In addition, the quality and volume of BDPs' restoration activities considerably enhanced the growing awareness – local, national and international – that the rich cultural heritage of Bhaktapur and of other important historical sites in Nepal deserves particular attention, especially when it is endangered by other, often conflicting forces of development and modernization.

The project has also proved that protection of old buildings and areas of architectural and historical interest is an important asset, both in the cultural and economic sense. As mentioned, in one of the restored buildings known as Kuthu Math, a National Brass and Bronze Museum has been established, and more recently the restored Pujari Math has been turned into a National Wood Carving Museum. In this way the monumental heritage has been used for promotion, protection and development of other cultural heritages, while also generating tourism revenues.

The most spectacular reconstruction was that of the *sattal* (rest house) in the middle of Taumadhi Square, in 1976. The old building was transformed into a café – the first and most visible adaptive re-use of a historical structure for tourism. (Theophile & Gutschow, 2003, p. 15) The Café Nayatapola, located in a traditional building, is another attraction of this courtyard. The square is dominated by the finely carved façade of a large private house belonging to the Dhaubhadel family.

Conservation should be a means to preserve traditional local skills and create new employment. The interaction between tourism and conservation should be made beneficial, avoiding both negative impacts from tourism as well as mere conservation of the prevailing backwardness. Care should be taken to keep cultural activities alive. It is vital that ancient buildings be given an active role in contemporary society. The BDP succeeded in preserving traditional local skills and creating new employment. It encouraged and gave employment to people of various crafts and disciplines, including brickmakers, woodcarvers, masons and carpenters. The primarily agrarian population of Bhaktapur also learnt that besides farming they can earn a livelihood from some alternative professions as well. The local people have benefited by these restored monuments by utilizing them for commercial, educational, recreational and other purposes. The BDP and its follow-on programmes have helped the city to attract more visitors. Among the various prestigious heritage conservation awards won is the UNESCO prize in 1998/1999, which has helped to establish Bhaktapur as a popular tourist destination.

After the termination of BDP there remained many other monuments waiting for repair, restoration and rehabilitation in the World Heritage Site of Bhaktapur. Among them the most important were the Cyasilin Mandap, the Bhairabnath Temple and the Palace of Fifty-five Windows. Let us look at how the reconstruction of the Cyasilin Mandap, or 'the pavilion of eight corners', came about. The government of Germany expressed its desire to reconstruct this pavilion as a token gift on the occasion of the state visit of Chancellor Helmut Kohl in July 1987. The official announcement was made during the state visit, in appreciation of Bhaktapur's unique quality of traditional urban space. The 17th-century Cyasilin Mandap, long considered a precious historical building, had been totally destroyed by the earthquake in 1934. Probably, it had originally been built as a viewing terrace from which members of the Bhaktapur court could observe the processions, seasonal rituals, and festivals of the urban community.

Art historians considered it as the beauty spot of Bhaktapur Durbar Square, but it was one of many monuments which the Rana Prime Ministers did not consider important to rebuild after the 1934 earthquake. Also the three-storey Harishankara/Krishna temple, the two-storey Puresvara Temple, the two-storey Tilmadhav Narayan temple and large portions of the palace area were left untouched. Some other monuments were restored but their architecture was drastically changed – such as the Silumahadeva Temple, whose shikhara tower was replaced by a gable roof, the three-storey Jaganath Temple, whose shrine was covered by a gable roof, and the Badrinath Temple, whose shikhara tower was replaced by a gable over the ground floor. (Gutschow & Hagmuller, 1991)

After the earthquake, the Ranas left four temples in the Durbar Square, making them one-storey makeshift buildings. Four other monuments were completely razed to the ground: the Cyasilin Mandap, built by King Jitamitra Malla (1663–87) probably in 1680, was one of them. A knee-high octagonal platform on which a tall stone inscription with poems about Nepal's six seasons composed by King Jitamitra Malla together with his prime minister in around AD

1680 has been preserved as a memory of this Mandap. Extensive research work to discover the remains of the carved artifacts of this structure found that they were being used in various structures in Bhaktapur and Kathmandu. Before rebuilding, detailed studies were done of photographs taken by Gustave Le Bon in 1885, Percy Brown in 1905, the collection of Giusseppi Tucci and the collection of the photographer Ganesh Chitrakar. To these were added engravings and watercolours made from drawings and notes of the Schlagintweit brothers, Henry Ambrose Oldfield (1880) and Daniel Wright in the mid-19th century and many others. During research, original components of the building were recovered, making possible an exact reconstruction of the exterior, with the proper proportions. The re-use of the pillars and beams crushed by the teeth of time has ensured the authentic character of the edifice: eight of twelve pillars, 30% of the lintel and six of sixteen capitals could be preserved. (Gutschow & Hagmuller, 1991, p.5.) The architect restorers had at least some authentic documents of the outer architecture of the Mandap, but none for the interior, where they used their knowledge for fabricating the inner settings. In their own words, this was their 'pure invention'.

The restorers had to face many difficulties and challenges in course of their work. The building that has now been completed is essentially a copy based largely on a 'creative design', as the outer appearance deviates clearly from the historical model in several details. To avoid 'historical falsification' and to give 'contemporary stamp' according to the Venice Charter, all modern materials such as steel beams and frames etc used in this monument have been made visible. (Gutschow & Hagmuller, 1991.)

Expressing his reactions on the reconstruction of the Cyasilin Mandap, Prof. Dr. Eduard F. Sekler has said: *I fully understood that from the urban designer's point of view the decision to reconstruct was understandable and commendable. But, at the same time from the point of view of the architectural historian and preservationist, I felt that the reconstruction clearly was a typical example of historic falsification: a new building that pretended to have survived from the time of its construction in the 17th century. The question here was: did the values of the urban designer deserve priority, or those of the historians/preservationist?'* He added: *reconstruction shall be undertaken only when such work is essential to reproduce a significant* *missing feature in a historic district or scene, and when a contemporary design solution is not acceptable*. In fact the Cyasilin Mandap was standing at the main courtyard of the Bhaktapur Durbar Square like a red *tika*-mark adorning the forehead of a beautiful lady. Its loss was very much felt by the local people for quite some time. (Sekler, 1992)

> The re-construction of the pavilion incorporated earthquake-strengthening measures to protect the top-heavy building from another quake. This led to the decision to introduce a rigid steel frame into the reconstructed historical building (Theophile & Gutschow, 2003, pp. 16–17).

Regarding the use of steel beams and concrete in this reconstruction project, heavy criticism came from some Nepalese architects and archaeologists, but when they understood that it was totally a reconstruction project with the help of some old sketches, they kept quiet. Also Article 9 of the Venice Charter says: *The process of restoration is a highly specialized operation. Its aim is to preserve and reveal the aesthetic and historic value of the monument and is based on respect for original material and authentic documents. It must stop at the point where conjecture begins, and in this case moreover any extra work, which is indispensable, must be distinct from the architectural composition and must bear a contemporary stamp*. Similarly Article 10: *Where traditional techniques prove inadequate, the consolidation of a monument can be achieved by the use of any modern technique for conservation and construction, the efficacy of which has been shown by scientific data and proved by experience*. The restoration in any case must be preceded and followed by an archaeological and historical study of the monument. Also we have to give the stamp of the time when we totally reconstruct any monument. Today, both locals and foreign visitors can appreciate this once-ruined Mandap.

In connection with the third SAARC Summit held in Nepal in 1987, numerous monuments in and around Bhaktapur Durbar Monument Zone were repaired. Among these was the terracotta temple of Lord Rameshwar situated to the south of the main courtyard. Still, many courtyards of medieval palaces are dilapidated and are awaiting major repairs, including the Mul Chowk.

In 1999–2000, the Krishna Mandir of the Bhaktapur palace complex was renovated. Indeed, since that time, Bhaktapur Municipality has been taking initiative to prepare a Master Plan for the conservation of the Bhaktapur Monument Zone (BMZ) but it has not yet been published. At Bhaktapur Monument Zone all that glitters is not gold, as some 59 houses have been built against the norms of the DOA. Still, in comparison to other two ancient palace squares, the BMZ and the area surrounding the old palace have not suffered much from encroachment by inappropriate tall buildings. Due to the efforts of the Bhaktapur Development Project, and to the fact of less development pressure than in Kathmandu and Patan, Bhaktapur has managed to retain much of its traditional townscape. Modern development is centred on the new roads to the north and south, rather than in the centre of the historic city.

Apart from public monuments, which at least fall under some form of legal protection and official responsibility, it is the private housing sector of Bhaktapur which is in danger and needs particular attention. Here we find a wide range of historically important buildings – representing the physical background, urban setting and coherent visual character of the town and its monumental sites. However, this private housing sector is not protected from illegal demolition and replacement. While such replacement and new housing development has been increasing for several years, it is inadequately controlled under existing regulations and their inefficient enforcement. If the current building boom continues unchecked, then only in a few years it will have changed and replaced the historic character of Bhaktapur forever – far more profoundly than all earthquakes have achieved hitherto.

In Bhaktapur Durbar Monument Zone we can also find examples of illegal and bad constructions, such as the building of Siva Guest-House, which has yet to get formal approval from the relevant authorities. The concrete building of Nepal Telcom behind the terracotta Rameshwar Temple is another such bad construction within the monument zone.

Although local regulations to control the height and style of new structures within the historic core area were proposed by the BDP in 1975, little attention was paid to this Western notion of townscape preservation. The scene began to change after the advent of democracy in 1990, when the absolute majority of the Nepal Workers and Peasants Party in Bhaktapur gave local authorities more power. In 1996, awareness of the city's tourism potential encouraged the municipal authorities to enforce strict building bylaws within the WHS, the boundaries of which were even extended in 1997.

Some examples can indicate that the picture is not entirely bleak. In 1997, Samanta Raj Sakya of Inacva, Bhaktapur, started to rebuild his house, but the ward chairman forced him to construct it according to the design permitted by the Municipality. The owner had wanted to rebuild with large windows, cantilever in the second floor, increasing ceiling heights and one more storey than permitted, but he was forced to abide by rules that could not accommodate any of these features. Similarly, when the house next to the Nyatapvala pagoda was rebuilt in 1998, the owner was forced to hide the reinforced concrete frame with traditional brick veneer.

The house renovated by Rabindra Puri, also known as Namuna Ghar (Model House) has not only encouraged the educated and aware residents of Bhaktapur but also shown that a good restoration or renovation can provide a nice, comfortable dwelling as well as gaining a respectable place in the world community. This Namuna Ghar was awarded UNESCO Heritage Award in 2004. The award recognizes the high quality of the restoration work as well as its model and trend-setting function within the historic settlements of the Kathmandu Valley (UNESCO, Kathmandu, 2006, p. 17).

In recent years a new pseudo-Newa style has emerged and dresses every new concrete frame structure with a variety of vaguely traditional details. This is especially true of the new shopping arcades in and around the Durbar Square, which have been built by affluent individuals to expand their tourist trade. Do these houses preserve the notion of historic environment?

In 1998, 'Visit Nepal Year', the municipality authorities and local politicians decided to construct new city gates at major access points to the town. Although primarily an urban beautification project, the new gates loosely recall the city's early fortifications, of which only one gate survives. The new gates are tourist attractions of sorts with historic connotations but different from any precedent in proportion, style, and scale. Except for the sale of entry tickets and checking tourists, these gates do not fulfil any other purpose. These gates, like the pseudo-Newa style structures mentioned above, demonstrate how a new architectural style related to tourism impacts in the historic city. On the one hand, the visual continuity of this revivalist style may be preferable to the more modern infirm projects of previous years, but the many compromises in historical detail, loss of authentic building fabric, and the relocation of families from their ancestral homes must be noted. The frightening uniformity of the new 'traditional' façades also contrasts with the richness of Bhaktapur's vernacular style, suggesting that strict guidelines are no panacea for historic town preservation. The story of Bhaktapur is representative of similar developments in the centres of Kathmandu and Patan also. WHS tourism offers an economic incentive to preserve, but is also inseparable from larger social and functional changes which cannot always be environmentally friendly (Theophile & Gutschow, 2003, pp. 23–24).

Since the 1990s, the local politicians of Bhaktapur have become very vocal and active in their campaign to get Bhaktapur recognized as a 'Cultural City'. Bhaktapur Municipality has organized seminars and meetings aiming at fulfilling this objective, and have invoked the law on Local Self-government (*Swayatta Shasan Ain*, BS 2055) and its accompanying regulation (*Swayatta Shasan Niyamabali*, BS 2056). These laws specify that if a municipality is in listed in the World Heritage List and if the government wishes to protect its historical and archaeological objects and art and culture it can be declared as a 'Cultural City'. The 9th five-year plan also states that within this plan period it will develop necessary provisions for declaring Bhaktapur as a 'Cultural City'. But the Ministry of Culture and the DOA have some reservations on this matter. Unless the Ancient Monument Preservation Act of BS 2013 is amended and a new provision for declaring a city as a cultural city is included, nothing can be done. If the DOA is willing to amend the law and include this new clause of declaring a city as a 'Cultural City', it will have to make some rules and regulations and develop some criteria. Moreover, once any other city in the nation fulfils these criteria, also that city has to be declared as a 'Cultural City'. Therefore this demand of Bhaktapur has been adjudged to be not so pressing for the time being. After all, nowhere else in the world has a country has declared a city as a 'Cultural City'. Will officially declaring Bhaktapur as a 'Cultural City' mean we are adding a new definition to the cultural heritage, or what? In fact Bhaktapur already occupies a unique position on the map of world cultural heritage. It is considered as a shining piece of solid gold – and no gold requires any artificial touching-up (Amatya, 2002b).

Bhaktapur Municipality has set an excellent example by levying tourist entry fees to the WHS since 1994. Considerable revenues have been gained, for use in the repair and restoration of monuments and sanitation of the city. Since November 1997, various important monuments have been face-lifted, repaired and re-roofed, among them the temples of Nyatapvala, Bhairabnath, Yakshvara, Dvarikanath and others. Some historic ponds, like the Siddha Pokhari, have been cleaned and rehabilitated. According to *The Sunday Post* (Kathmandu), 30 November 1997, the municipality has ambition of making Bhaktapur the cleanest city in the country, and, by conserving and protecting the city's cultural heritage, developing it into the cultural capital of Asia.

Bhaktapur Durbar Square Ca.1921.

Palace of Fifty-five Windows, Bhaktapur and ruins, 1934 (Courtesy: Images of Nepal, page 103).

Recent photograph of Bhaktapur Durbar Square

Batsala Temple and Pashupati Temple, Bhaktapur Durbar Square (1975).

Bhagwati Temple, Bhaktapur Durbar Square, before 1979.

Bhagwati Temple and Fasi Dega (Shiva Temple) in the background. Totally destroyed by the earthquake of 1934, only the base of the original structure remains. (Courtesy: Collection of Prof. Tucci, ISMEO, Rome)

Destruction of Bhaktapur city by the earthquake of 1934: Nyatapvala Temple in the background.

Taumadhi Square of Bhaktapur in ruins after the earthquake of 1934. The Bhairav Temple was reduced to a pile of rubble.

Nyatapvala Temple, Bhaktapur, damaged by the earthquake of 1934.

Nyatapvala Temple before the earthquake of 1934. (Courtesy: Collection of Prof. Tucci, ISMEO, Rome)

(Courtesy: Department of Archaeology)

Nyatapvala Temple of Bhaktapur

Palace of 55 Windows, under renovation in 2006.
Bhaktapur Durbar Square, ca.1921. (Courtesy: Department of Archaeology)

Taumadhi Square of Bhaktapur, after the reconstruction of the Bhairav Temple in 1990.

Dattatraya Temple, Bhaktapur

Fasi Dewal after the earthquake of 1934.

Woodcarvers in progress

Bhairav Temple of Taumadhi Square, Bhaktapur before renovation in 1995 (Courtesy: Department of Archaeology)

Bhairav Temple after renovation in 1996 (Courtesy: Department of Archaeology)

Sketch of Bhaktapur Durbar Square from Gustava Le Bon, Voyage Au Nepal, 1883 to 1886, p. 35.

Sketch of 55 window Palace from Gustava Le Bon, Voyage Au Nepal, 1883 to 1886, p. 39.

6
Conservation of Swayambhu Monument Zone

> Whoever here, after the stupa due to age has collapsed or otherwise deteriorated, undertakes works of restoration will have a perfect body devoid of all disease and eventually will obtain the *Dharmakaya* Truth-Body, most excellent in every aspect.
>
> – *Svayambhupurana*

Building, restoring and renovating a stupa has always brought merit, this most essential of preconditions for a favourable re-birth. In more senses than one, the form stands for the essence of the Buddhist faith. Renovations of *chaityas* have been regarded in the same way, with the merit that accrued from such work being all the higher, the greater the religious importance of the monument repaired. The Swayambhu Mahachaitya, or Great Stupa, with its high prestige among Newa Buddhists and beyond, has greatly benefited from this belief; indeed, in an essential way it has contributed to its continued survival (Kolver, 1992, pp. 38.)

Swayambhu Mahachaitya, one of the World Heritage Sites of the Kathmandu Valley, is the most revered Buddhist stupa in all Nepal. Situated atop a hill in the west of Kathmandu, Swayambhu Mahachaitya is the most prominent monument of the Kathmandu Valley, visible from all directions. The tree-covered hillside has been inhabited by monkeys since ancient days, so this monument is also known to tourists as the Monkey Temple.

The historical origins of this Great Stupa are obscure. Historians believe that the Kushans who migrated into this Valley from India might have built the stupa around the first or second century AD. Legend says that all the Buddhas who have taken human form, including Bipaswi, Sikkhi, Biswombhu, Krukuchhand, Kanakamuni, Kasyapa and Sakyamuni, have come here to pay homage to the Swayambhu, 'The Self-Originated Divine Illumination'. Later on great Buddhist teachers and philosophers like Guru Padmasambhava, Atisa Deepankar, Bikshu Dharma Swami and many others have visited Swayambhu Mahachaitya to pay homage.

There are two main approaches leading to the Great Stupa – one from the east and the other from the south. On the eastern side, the stone stairway is very steep, consisting of some 365 steps. At the base of this stairway there are three big Buddha statues; then follow stone figures of animals – pairs of royal lions, elephants, horses, peacocks and mythological garudas, which are considered the vehicles of the five Dhayani (meditation) or Celestial Buddhas: Vairochana, Akshobhya, Ratnasambhava, Amitabha and Amoghasiddhi, respectively.

The Swayambhu Mahachaitya premises have numerous monuments and objects of historical, cultural, and religious value. The main Mahachaitya or stupa is a huge dome, roughly 50 m^2 in area, in the form of a flattened hemisphere. Around the periphery of the circular base, the *garva* (womb), are installed the five Celestial Buddhas with their respective female counterparts: Vairochana (Vajradhateswari Pragayaramita), Akshobhya (Saptalochani Tara), Ratnasambhava (Mamki Tara), Amitabha (Paddura Tara) and Amoghasiddhi (Arya Tara). Above the dome stands a golden column in the centre or *harmika;* on each of its four sides there is a pair of penetrating eyes symbolizing wisdom, love, kindness and compassion. Right above the eyes on the *toranas* or tympanums are marked the images of four Buddhas and other Buddhist deities. Above this we see *cakravali* or the thirteen glittering divisions called *trayadasha bhuvana* – the thirteen heaven or the Bodhisattva worlds. Atop the Great Stupa there is a *chhatra* (canopy, parasol) and a *gajura,* or pinnacle.

In the vicinity are numerous monuments of importance. These include the shikhara-style temples of Pratappur and Anantapur built by King Pratap Malla; Basupur, with the image of the goddess Basundhara, the bestowal of prosperity; Vayupur, the god of wind; and the artistic golden temple of the goddess Ajima or Harati, protector of children. Harati is a tantric goddess, worshipped by the Nepalese as the mother protector. Then there is Agnipur, which is supposed to protect against fire. Other monuments include Nagapur, the shrine dedicated to the serpent god, and Shantipura, a shrine dedicated to the sky. It is believed that there are 27 compartments under the ground floor of this shrine. Accepting this popular belief, King Pratap Malla of Kathmandu once boldly entered one of the compartments and brought out a manuscript written with the blood of serpents, to drive out drought. And indeed, soon a very heavy rain ensued, and the people were saved from the drought.

The Swayambhu Mahachaitya is a veritable treasure house of valuable artifacts like bronze and stone images and miniature *chaityas*. Some very beautiful bronze statues stand on the western side of the stupa, in front of the Harati Temple, on top of stone pillars. On the eastern side, on the top of a Mandala, there is a massive *vajra* or thunderbolt. This golden *vajra* – known as *dorje* in Tibetan – is the very symbol of Vajrayana Buddhism, or 'the Path of the Thunderbolt'. In the vicinity of the Great Stupa there are Tibetan, Bhutanese and Nepalese *viharas* and *gumbas*, as well as a museum where numerous religious manuscripts and bronze and stone images of both Buddhist and Hindu deities are kept. Indeed, the entire site is a unique open-air museum, unparalleled elsewhere in the world.

The Swayambhu Mahachaitya is the most sacred shrine of Mahayana Buddhism in Nepal. In 1989 His Majesty's Government with the co-operation of German government prepared the Swayambhunath Conservation Masterplan. Since then, the government together with the Swayambhu Mahasamiti, a local NGO, have been vigorously carrying out conservation, repair and development activities in the monument zone. Foreign tourists have to pay an entrance fee to this Great Stupa. But unfortunately it has not yet been possible to keep this World Heritage Site as clean and peaceful as most Buddhist pilgrimage sites elsewhere.

Hindus and Buddhists from all over the world consider the Swayambhu Mahachaitya as a centre of pilgrimage of utmost importance. It has served as a place of great religious synchronism between Hinduism and Buddhism since ancient times. From early morning, devotees pay homage to this stupa and its surrounding deities, with deep faith. Their numbers swell on special occasions like full-moon days, half-moon days and the first day of the month. The sacred month of *Gunla*, which falls in August/September, attracts even more devotees. At the full moon in March, and then in May, the day when Sakyamuni Buddha was born, gained enlightenment and finally passed into *mahaparinirvana,* people from all walks of life visit this auspicious shrine.

The history of conservation of Swayambhu Mahachaitya is very old. According to the chronicle *Swayambhu Purana*, King Vrishadev, the great-grandfather of King Manadev, had constructed the Great Stupa in the early 5th-century AD, following the advice of Bhikshu Shanti Sheel, on the exact spot where since time immemorial the self-originated great eternal beacon 'Swayambhunath' had been in existence. King Manadev decorated the Mahachaitya with a finial or *chattra*. The *Tang Annals* of China mention that in AD 657, Chinese Ambassador Wang Huien Tse offered gifts to this Great Stupa on behalf of his emperor. Sometime in the 12th-century, Sakya Bikshu Maitri Chandra restored the great stupa and replaced its *yashi (yasti)* or central ceremonial pole. According to the *Red Annals,* a chronicle compiled in the 14th-century, a certain Jo-btsun s Pras-pa renovated the Swayambhu Mahachaitya when he came to Nepal, between 1215 and 1230. For this purpose he cut the tree for the new *yasti* in the forest of Singa, in the environs of Nuwakot to the north of the Kathmandu Valley. When the renovation was finished, he set up a new *chattra,* whitewashed the rebuilt *chaitya* and installed a 'long stone' – presumably an inscription. After Jo-btsun s Pras-pa had been honoured with gifts by the king and distinguished citizens of Kathmandu, he set off towards Tibet, and is said to have died along the way, at a place called Rashamase.

According to Tibetan sources, the Swayambhunath Mahachaitya was renovated in the second half of the 13th-century: 'After a certain time the mast there broke. Sakya bzang-po donated three large *dronas* and 50 ounces of gold. The Kalyanamitras from dBus and gtsang, the *bares* from Nepal, (and) the *thakuras* from India having donated much wealth, the (new) mast was set up by lamas from Central Tibet, father and son'. Sakya bzang-po was the first chief administrator of the whole of Tibet, answerable directly to the Mongolian leadership. Since he held office from 1264 to 1270, it is likely that the renovation of Swayambhu was carried out (or at least initiated) at some point during this period. (Ehrhard, 1991.)

In the mid-14th century, troops of the Muslim invader Shumshud-din-Iliyas plundered and destroyed the Great Stupa. The first major restoration was carried out by a Mahapatra of Kathmandu named Rajharsha Vallok, as commanded by King Jayarjun Dev and Jayasthiti Malla, according to an inscription located at Swayambhunath. Further, according to this inscription, following the hoisting of the precious *chattra*, the renovated stupa was re-consecrated in October 1372, with an extended fire ritual of one hundred thousand oblations (*laksahuti)*, lasting four days and four nights. In addition to the *chattra* and the thirteen gilded rings (*cakravali*) rising above the *harmika*, a crystal vessel and a staff surmounted by a gem and studded with jewels were offered to the *chaitya*. A golden (that is, golden-plated) finial (*suvarnakalasa*), banners, and golden struts were also provided. Presumably, these donations had become necessary because the jewels and gold parts of the previous structure had been plundered by the troops of the Muslim invader. Before these newly donated parts were installed atop the *chaitya* together with the aforementioned *chattra*, they were taken around Kathmandu in a big festal procession that lasted likewise four days and four nights. This inscription also gives the names of the priests, the astrologer, the jeweller (Sriman Candra) who made what probably served as the new *cudamani,* and two woodworkers (Sthapit Bharo and his nephew Jayaram Bharo) who were presumably in charge of fitting the *yasti* and possibly of rebuilding the chaitya as a whole (von Rospatt, 2001& H. Sakya, 1978).

According to an inscription located inside the courtyard at Itumbhal, the Mahamantri or Chief Minister Madan Ram Vardhan had restored the Swayambhu Mahachitya and the temple of Harati Ajima (also known as Yakjati) during the reign of King Jayasthiti Malla (AD 1382–95). The chronicle *Gopala Raja Vamsabali* also credits King Jayasthiti Malla with being one of the restorers of the Great Stupa (H. Sakya, 1978, p. 144; &. S. Sakya, 2005, pp. 1–2).

Shortly after this, work was done on the Mahachitya by King Jyotir Malla and his son Yaksha Malla. In 1413, King Joytir Malla restored the Great Stupa and also beautified it. In this restoration work he was assisted by Mahapandita Sariputra. According to Tibetan sources, 'the king of Nepal, Sri Jyotirmalladeva, superintended and, after having praised the assembled *bares* in an official writing, called together the craftsmen under his charge.' It seems that the main person who actually carried out the renovation was not a Newa, but Mahapandita Sakya-Sri Sariputra, the celebrated abbot of Bodhgaya. It is he who is credited with having set up the new *yasti* to replace the previous one that had broken. This the abbot did when passing through Nepal on his way to the Chinese emperor, who had invited him to the Ming court. Mahapandita Sariputra apparently used funds provided by the Chinese emperor for whitewashing the dome of Swayambhu. Thus this renovation attests not only to continuous links between Buddhists of India and Nepal, but also to the fame of Swayambhu in a place as distant as the Chinese capital. (von Rospatt 2001, p. 203.)

Tibetan sources also mention that the Tibetan holy man gTsang-smyon Heruka (1452–1507) was called upon to undertake the renovation of Swayambhunath Mahachaitya by King Ratna Malla (AD 1484–1520) and his ministers in 1504, and that this work was completed after three years. According to the biography of Heruka written in 1547, after receiving permission from King Ratna Malla, he and his disciples started to raise the necessary funds from among Tibetans and Nepalese. It is also mentioned that at that time the 13 rings (*cakravali*) and the superstructure above were replaced, but not the central pole – the *yasti*. In this renovation project the workers were no doubt men from the Valley, but the undertaking was clearly in the hands of Tibetans. The lamas not only supervised the renovation work but also carried out necessary rituals, including the re-consecration *(rab gnas)* of the Swayambhu Mahachaitya.

Another Tibetan source says nearly twenty years after the renovation by Heruka, the Great Stupa was demolished by the Magar troops of Mukunda Sen, king of the western Nepali kingdom of Palpa, in March 1526. They plundered the Mahachaitya, taking away the gilded rings and *chattra,* and then tried to set fire to the remaining structure, thereby disfiguring but not seriously damaging it. The *chaitya* had once more become impaired and needed to be rebuild. 'Ha-btsun Rin-chen rNam-rgyal (1473–1557), a disciple of Heruka, took the initiative and began renovation work in 1530. A new *yasti* was erected and the superstructure was rebuilt with the tiers, the *chattra* and the finial. Perhaps because of scarcity of funds, this renovation went on for a period of almost ten years, so that the Great Stupa was not re-consecrated until 1539/40, during the reign of King Amara Malla (1529–60). It seems that 'Ha-btsun's funds were so meagre that he only covered parts of the *harmika* and none of the rings with gilded copper sheets. At any rate, the western and northern side of the *harmika* and the 13 tiers were covered with such sheets by his disciple sKyid-grong-gnas Rab-'byams-pa Byams-pa Phun-tshogs (1503–81) thirty years later in 1570 – an event which was followed by another consecration 1572 (von Rospatt, 2001, pp. 206–07).

Some sixty years after the installation of a new central pole by 'Ha-btsun, this *yasti* had become old and weakened, so extensive renovation including the replacement of the *yasti* was carried out from 1591 to 1595. In the month of Caitra in NS 711 (April 1591) the tree for the central pole of the stupa was brought from Nuwakot as usual. The following year, in June 1592, various neighbourhoods of Kathmandu took it in turns to tow the *yasti,* which arrived some six weeks later at the top of Swayambhu. Work continued only after an interval of a year and half, in December 1593, with the fabrication of new rings up at Swayambhu. A further two months later, in February 1594, the stupa was de-consecrated by extracting the divine essence (*nyasa*) and then quickly dismantled, so that exactly two months later, on the 11th day of the waxing fortnight of Caitra (April 1594), the new *yasti* could be raised. Within the next six months the stupa was rebuilt, and on the second day of the waxing fortnight of Aswin (October 1594) the divine essence was re-transferred from its temporary abode in a sacred vessel where it had been kept. Half a year later, preparations for the consecration rituals began. These were performed in the following month within the framework of an extended fire ritual lasting twelve days and eleven nights. The renovation was concluded in May 1595.

Very soon, however, the Mahachaitya was struck by lightning and had to be renovated all over again. In 1601, King Siva Singh Malla allocated the responsibility for this work to a wealthy friend,

Sakyabhiksu Jayaraksa (also known as Jayaharsa). For this renovation the *yasti* was brought from Kapilasa near Nuwakot, arriving at Swayambhu in February 1602. Only five months later, the divine essence was extracted. The dismantling of the stupa and the subsequent raising of the new *yasti* took seven months. The consecration was completed exactly one year later, in February 1604, with a fire ritual that lasted five days and four nights. A *thyasapu* or manuscript (available at the National Archives of Nepal, Reel No. E1874/2) provides a detailed description of how the renovation works were carried out by Jayaraksa and the role played by people of various localities of Kathmandu (von Rospatt, 2001, pp. 209–13).

In NS 741 (AD 1621) during the reign of King Laxmi Narasimha Malla (1619–41) the Swayambhu Mahachaitya was completely renovated, and again in 1637, under the same monarch. According to a *thyasapu* in March 1637 the *chaitya* was de-consecrated after the new *yasti* had arrived at Swayambhu. Within less than two months the stupa was dismantled and the old central pole extracted. In May 1637 the new *yasti* was erected. The rebuilding then commenced, which took 14 months to complete. In June 1638 the thirteen rings and the superstructure were installed. In July, three weeks after work on the superstructure was concluded, the four Buddha statues and the finials for their niches were set up after they had been taken around the town in a procession. Two days later, the divine essence was transferred from its temporary abode in the *nyasa ghata,* or sacred vessel, back into the *chaitya*. But only in December 1639 were all the final consecration rites completed. The main donors, apart from local citizens, were King Laxmi Narasimha Malla, his son crown prince Pratap Malla and one Chandra Bharo. (See von Rospatt, 2001, pp. 213–15.) King Pratap Malla (AD 1661–94) not only renovated the stupa but also added the two beautiful shikhara temples Pratappur and Anantapur, and the Dharmadhatu Mandala with the massive gilded *vajra* on the top.

In 1629/30, the Syamarpa Lama (the Zhva-dmar-pa) came to Nepal and donated gilded shields *(torana)* for the four niches at Swayambhu. According to Hem Raj Sakya, in 1565 the Mahapatras of Patan had replaced part of the finial.

In about 1681–83 after completing restoration work at Boudhanath, Rang-rig ras-pa, a yogi from Spiti (in the Himalayas of today's northwestern India) offered 32 ounces of gold to the King Parthivendra Malla with the request to finance with this the renovation of Swayambhu which had become necessary in 'connection with the statues of the four cardinal directions'. In the following year, before any efforts to start the renovation had got underway, the *yasti* 'broke and tilted left'. In fact this was the heinous act of a deranged man who climbed to the top of the stupa at night and dismantled the pinnacle along with the *chudamani,* which fell down and broken into pieces. Though the rite of begging for forgiveness was performed nine days later, it is possible that this act of de-consecration had marred the *chaitya* so much that its renewal was considered necessary. In 1681, renovation work began. In April the divine essence of the *chaitya* was extracted. After the de-consecration, it took three weeks before the dismantling of the uppermost part began. When the bowl-shaped crystal was taken down in May 1681 the two kings Parthivendra Malla and Mahipatendra Malla came for *darsan.* After several months, the *harmika* had been dismantled and the *yasti* protruding from the dome had been cut, and the dome was dismantled. Surprisingly, within only a week, in November 1681 the new central pole was raised. Again after a halt of some months the setting up of the thirteen rings began in April 1682. In May 1682 began the installation of the four Buddha statues in their niches in the dome. Then the *chattra* was affixed atop the *chaitya* and duly consecrated in the presence of the king. In June 1682 the finials had been installed atop the *chaitya,* and above the four niches in the dome, the divine essence was transferred from its temporal abode back into the newly rebuilt *chaitya.* Finally, in December 1682 the final consecration ceremonies were initiated.

In NS 834 (AD 1714) King Bhaskar Malla and the queen mother Bhuwan Laxmi restored the Mahachaitya, which was in a dilapidated condition due to rain and wind. Also this time all necessary rituals were performed before, during and after the restoration. A detailed description of this restoration can be found in the manuscript '*Swayambhu Chaitya Prasthapan Barnan*' available at the National Archives of Nepal. According to this source, in May/June 1710, before starting the work, *Chhema Puja* (pacification ritual, begging for forgiveness) was performed. At the same time at Shantipur,

Samaya Chakra Puja and *Ganachakra Puja,* various types of tantric worship were performed. On the third day the divine essence *(nyasa* or soul or life) of the Swayambhu Mahchaitya was removed by performing *Hom,* the sacred fire ritual. The sacred texts were read. In a big vessel or *khashi,* five persons poured water from five jars as an offering to different deities. Two cows were honoured: they were decorated with golden horns and silver on their toes, then were covered with white cloth and given five different kinds of food, *panchabriha,* to eat. After that other necessary worship was performed, and the pitcher in which the soul or life of Swayambhu was kept was brought. While taking out the soul of the deity, all elements such as the *phikha deo, tara deo, galatuki,chaku, yasti, phatakibata* (crystal vessal) and *chattra* or parasol were tied with the sacred thread called *panchabisati.* Then the pitcher in which the soul was to be kept was placed there. Making a place for the sacred fire or *panchasali,* ritual worshipping was done at Shantipur. Later, the *phatakibata*, a sacred vessel or crystal bowl, was removed from the stupa. Then in Pousha NS 831 (winter AD 1711) the central pole was transported. Ritual worship was made by offerings from the king, and on the fourth day the central pole reached Swayambhu. The priest of Swayambhu offered food to all those involved on that day. Once the *yasti* or central pole had arrived at Shantipur it was welcomed by the senior priest of Swayambhu and his three helpers. In winter 1712, to remove the *Chawukakhat Jwala* the carpenter had to worship it: and to remove the *Gartuki* ritual worshipping was done by Mulacharya, Upadhaya and Karmacharya. To excavate the area from where the central pole would be joined together with a new pole, two ploughs *(kokicha)* were wrapped in gold. At an auspicious time the dome was dismantled and necessary rituals were performed at Shantipur. The old and rotten central pole was removed and burnt, and the new central pole was towed from Agnipur and placed in the dome, accompanied by various rituals and worship. The Karmacharya recited the holy book *Pancharaksha* in front of the main deity. Royal offerings were brought. Many classical religious dances were performed, such as *Kumha Pykhan* and *Daitya Pykhan, Raja Pykhan,* and various musical instruments were played. With a big procession, King Bhaskar Malla arrived at the site. After performing all necessary rituals, attempts were made to raise the central pole, but without success. King Bhaskar Malla and the Queen Mother Bhuwan Laxmi and numerous other dignitaries were watching the ceremony, but the central pole could not be raised even after the fourth attempt. Only after prayers had been offered to numerous deities did the central pole become straight. On the spot where the pole was erected, ceremonial flags were offered – first by the leader of the pulling team, then by the *salamis* or Manandhar clan, who were responsible for pulling the pole, and finally by the king himself. The pole was offered various types of traditional sweets, such as *yomari*, *gomadhi* and *chaku madhi*. After the pole had successfully been erected, the water pitcher was given to the king and the image of Sri Laxmi and Yaksha Yakshni presented to the queen mother. After four days, base plate of the king post was joined from the four sides and the carpenter *(karmi)* was honoured by giving him *betali* or crown cap of cloth. Then after five days, the ritual on the occasion of installing the beams or *nigha* was performed. Beams were installed inside the dome from four corners and the dome was repaired. Then, after various rituals had been performed, pillars, beams, rings or *chakuli* were also worshipped. The *chakuli* or wooden rings or *chakrabali* offered by people from various localities were installed there, including the *chakuli* offered by King Bhaskar Malla. The *chattra* and the *pharkibata* (crystal vessel) were reinstalled atop the *chaitya* and consecrated. In such a way, all the elements of the holy structure were constructed and sited in their proper places in the stupa, and ritual worship was performed. Then the frills or *halampau* (tympanum) of the west, east, south, and north were emplaced. To put the crystal vessel above the *chakrabali,* scaffolding was erected amidst much pomp. The sacred vessel was taken to the palace, where it was welcomed and was offered worship by the king; then it was taken around the city in procession and brought back to Swayambhu. In spring 1713, the casting of bronze images of Pancha Buddha was done, donated by the king and the queen mother. Finally, the bronze images of Akshobhya, Ratnasambhava, Amitabha, and Amoghasiddhi were taken around the city, brought back and emplaced in niches, their proper place at Swayambhu.

In 1751, during the reign of King Jaya Prakash Malla, the Swayambhu Mahachaitya was renovated jointly by Tibetans and Newas on the initiative of the Tibetan Nying-ma-pa lama Ka-thog

Rig-'dzin Tshe-dbang Nor-bu. It is said that, after returning from Tibet in 1748 he noted that the *harmika* above the dome of Swayambhu had collapsed, and found that the *chaitya* had been in a state of disrepair for some time. He then met King Jaya Prakash and requested him to have repairs done immediately, because to leave it as it was would be inauspicious for the whole world. Ultimately it was decided that the king should be in charge and the people should assume responsibility as before, while the lamas would merely be 'helpers'. But in practice the Lama Norbo himself directed this renovation, Newa priests performed rituals, the *bares* of Semgu (Swayambhu) functioned as *jajmans* and the various localities of Kathmandu assumed responsibility for the those part of the *chaitya* and the rituals they traditionally took care of. But, due to the Gorkha incursions into the Kathmandu Valley, Lama Norbo was ordered by the Dalai Lama to go to Ladakh to mediate between the warring factions, and renovation work was suspended for several years. In 1754, Lama Norbu met the Gorkha king and sought his help to obtain a *yasti* from Nuwakot. But the *yasti* did not arrived on the outskirts of Kathmandu till March 1757. In the meantime, Lama Norbu left Kathmandu for Tibet to raise more funds for the renovation, first entrusting his disciple bsTan-'dzin rdo-rje (Dorji) to continue the work. Lama Norbu died at Kyirong on his way to Tibet. Under the initiative of Lama Dorji in March 1757 the stupa was de-consecrated and dismantled, then swiftly rebuilt within seven months. By October that year the rebuilding was finished, and the divine essence could be transferred back into place. The stupa was twice consecrated, by Newa and by Tibetan traditions. In May/June 1758 the final consecration rituals were performed by Newa priests and the renovation was completed at last (von Rospatt, pp. 221–28). Hem Raj Sakya (1978, pp. 244–57) has described interestingly how much money and precious metals like gold and silver were used during this restoration. Old and used silver and gold were separated and re-used, adding more. A total of 1382 *dharnis* (one *dharni* is 2.5 kg) of silver, and 3,344 *tolas* (or 39 kg) of gold were used. For other necessary materials including edibles, 43,639 rupees were spent, and further expenses came in addition.

After the Shah (Gorkha) conquest of the Kathmandu Valley in the late 18th-century, a major renovation of the Great Stupa was undertaken from 1814 to 1816. According to Tibetan sources, the *yasti* had started to lean to the left in 1812 and finally tumbled down in 1813 after a heavy storm. A new *yasti* was located and brought to Kathmandu, but it took two years until it arrived at Swayambhu, early in 1817. In this renovation work some Bhutanese lamas assisted the Shah king. The latter granted them some land next to Mahachaitya and the right to erect a Bhutanese temple, which was duly built in 1819. The Bhutanese lama took part in building up the *chaitya,* deposited sacred objects in it, offered a brocade pennant to *yasti*, and performed rituals. Some local Newa merchants *(sahus)* with trade connections in Tibet also supported this project with funds and materials: Sahu Srikrishna sponsored the copper covering for the upper part of the *yasti*, while Visnudhara had the statue of Ratnasambhava in the southern niche of the dome gilded.

Twelve days after the *yasti* arrived at Swayambhu, began the preparatory rituals of begging forgiveness and empowerment for the extraction of the divine essence. In February 1817 the de-consecration ritual was accomplished. Within the next two weeks the stupa was dismantled. In the following three weeks the remainder of the old *yasti* was removed and the new one was raised. In the course of the next two and half months, the stupa was built up again. After the last ring had been fixed in June, the pinnacle above the rings – including the honourific *chattra* but excluding the finial and the crest-jewel, which were offered only at the conclusion of the extended consecration – was installed and the Buddha statues were set up in their niches. Thus, only four months after the de-consecration, this dismantling and subsequent rebuilding of the Great Stupa were finished.

Not only Tibetan lamas and Newa merchants but also the government was actively involved in this renovation. The government requisitioned 2,100 men – 700 each from Kathmandu, Patan and Bhaktapur – for pulling the *yasti* from Nuwakot to Swayambhu. A high-ranking, prominent government official, the Karpardar Bhotu Pande, was in charge of this, and in the process spent many days and nights in the rugged wilderness between Nuwakot and the Valley. After the procurement of the *yasti* and before the dismantling of the *chaitya,* the king sent Kaji Bakhtabar Singh Basnyet and Dittha Laxam to Swayambhu for consultations with the priests and the *semgu bares*. Moreover, the king – that is, his government – took care not only of the uppermost ring, as the monarch traditionally does, but also of the tenth and eleventh tiers when the traditional sponsors of these parts failed to carry out their obligation. Furthermore, when the gilded struts that are fashioned as flower garlands (or frills) and support the uppermost *gajura* were damaged shortly after the renovation had been completed, the government assumed responsibility for renewing the finial, which entailed replacing the *chattra*. Thus the necessary rituals were carried out specifically in the king's name, with no lesser person than the Kaji Bakhtabar Singh Basnyat acting in his stead as *jajman*. Moreover, at the consecration of the new *chattra*, the monarch's sword was present as his proxy.

Exactly what happened to the Great Stupa in the earthquake of 1834 is not known, but during the time of Prime Minister Jung Bahadur Rana (1846–77), three artisans were brought from China in order to repair the stupa (Regmi, 1976, p. 71). In NS 1028 (1908) the Marmey Lakhan Gumba – the Bhutanese Gumba – was totally destroyed by fire. Its restoration was completed in 1915.

The last major renovation of the Swayambhu Mahachaitya started in 1918. In NS 1037 (1917) as desired by Shakya Sri Lama of Tibet and under the direction of Duppa Lama of Bhutan, a wealthy Newa merchant named Dhama Sahu took the initiative to have the stupa renovated. Donations were to come from various sources, but Dhama Sahu was determined to complete the work even if he had to spend all his savings. In fact, he managed to raise funds not only from common devotees (supposedly some 75,000 Nepalese rupees), but also from the Dalai Lama (10,000 Nepalese rupees) and the king of Sikkhim (7,000 Indian rupees). Besides, many wealthy local people and the government had also helped this project with money and materials. The renovation work was accomplished within less than four months, although work with wood and copper for the new rings and other parts of the superstructure had already started in August/September of the preceding year. All the necessary rituals from the beginning to the end of the project were carried out in both Newa and the Tibetan traditions. Since the *yasti* was not replaced, the dome and *harmika* were not taken apart. However, the structure above was dismantled, the wood burnt according to percept, and the metals presumably melted down and recycled. Thus – in accordance with the concept of renovation as replacement rather than repair – the rings, the honourific parasol and all remaining superstructure except for the crest-jewel and crystal, were newly built. It seems that the new parts were more lavishly made than heretofore, and that some decorative elements were executed in gilded copper rather than, as previously, in simple cloth. Moreover, the niches were entirely renewed, and, for the first time, prayer wheels were added around the base of the dome. Another major change was the replacement of the statue of Vairochana, which had been slightly smaller than other Buddha statues in the niches and had displayed its specific *mudra* incorrectly. During this renovation the main stupa was enlarged and strengthened and many new decorative elements were added. At the same time, Pratappur and Anantapur were also restored. Ultimately the stupa was re-consecrated in separate ceremonies, according to Newa and Tibetan traditions. The renovation was completed in Ashad in NS 1041 (AD 1921). This was the last major restoration work done at Swayambhu Mahachaitya.

Major repairs will always be necessary at periodic intervals. The Swayambhu Mahachaitya has one fundamental difficulty: the heavy superstructure, and particularly the central pole *(yasti)* which runs through nearly the whole building, including the tiers. This must be a single trunk, some 22-m. in length (48 cubits 7 fingers). The upper end, where the pole is joined to the brickwork, is the danger point: this is where moisture will seep in and cause the wood to rot. As the tiers rest upon their own system of supports and are nowhere affixed to the *yasti,* an intact central pole is vital to the stupa for spiritual more than for technical reasons. When it is changed, the entire superstructure has to be dismantled, and the dome itself has to be opened. Then the old pole is extracted and cremated, and its ashes disposed of with solemn pomp: a procession takes them to the twelve holy sites (*tirthas*) of the Valley where they are immersed in the waters. Inserting a new *yasti*, then, is not so very far from building a new stupa: and the records show even parts that one would presume could have been re-used have instead been replaced. None of these, however, was ever given the honours accorded to the central pole: they were nothing but parts of a building, while the *yasti* had a life of its own (Kolver, 1992).

Suffering the ravages of time and storm, fire and earthquake, war and plunder, Swayambhu Mahachaitya has, with each significant repair, been modified to conform to the then existing doctrinal development. In each instance, however, in accordance with the tenets of stupa building everywhere, the original, primitive monument was not to have been replaced, but merely encased. Be this as it may, a great many restorations, renovations and repairs have been carried out at Swayambhu in the course of centuries, each of which must have occasioned certain further modifications or elaborations in the monument and its vicinity. Since the establishment of the Department of Archaeology (DOA) in BS 2018 (AD 1961) numerous small-scale restoration activities and infrastructure development works have been carried out at Swayambhu Monument Zone, from both the government and non-governmental sectors.

The Swayambhu Mahachaitya is one of the outstanding monuments of Asian culture: its inclusion in UNESCO's World Heritage List offers independent and impartial testimonial to this fact. And here due mention should be made of the help rendered by UNESCO and the World Heritage Committee, when landslides threatened the Swayambhu Hill in summer 1978. In August that year, the southeastern slope of Swayambhu was disrupted by landslide as a result of heavy monsoon rains. This caused great concern, as it was feared that both the stupa and the two eastern shikhara temples (Prattapur and Anantapur) were threatened by collapse. On the request of the government, emergency assistance was granted by UNESCO and the World Heritage Committee to save one of the most valued heritages of mankind. Nepal received the expert services of Mr. E. Kojan and Mr. Edward J. Cording for consolidating and counteracting further damage to the hill. A UNESCO mission under Mr. Kojan, dispatched immediately to analyse the situation, produced recommendations for the drainage of the slope and its stabilization by rock bolting. The drainage scheme was installed the following year, but the government of Nepal requested further investigations as to the suitability of the proposed rock bolting system. To avert the risk of further damage, the buildings immediately to the south of the Anantapur temple were torn down. The drainage of the slope was improved to prevent water from infiltrating from the pavement level and to relieve water pressures in the slope. The vertical cracks on the foundation walls of the Anantapur were repaired and strengthened by new bricks and cement mortar. Reinforced horizontal concrete beams were installed in the brick foundation of the temple walls. Loosened bricks that had not provided any significant support for the temple were removed. In December 1980, UNESCO expert Edward J. Cording made an evaluation of the southeastern slope. In his recommendations he clearly stated that movements on the southeastern slope had not caused significant damage to any historical structure at the top of the slope. As per his recommendations, survey level points or settlement points were established in 60 places, and the Survey Department was given responsibility for monitoring them. Piezometers to measure water levels were established; in addition, monthly rainfall records were established and the quantity of water coming out of the drains was measured and reported. During Cording's second mission in December 1981, an evaluation of slope conditions in other areas of the Swayambhu site was also conducted. According to Edward Cording, the most practical and economical way to minimize future slope movements and damage to structures is to keep new structures away from the edge of steep slopes, and to place foundations for new structures below recent fill materials. But when the local people demanded the reconstruction of *dyocchen* (the family divinity of the local inhabitants of Swayambhu) and the small temple of Vasundhara Devi, both of which had been demolished during the crisis, it took some time to solve this problem. After some discussion, all concerned parties reached a compromise, and the god house was built. The heavy old concrete walls were removed from the slope, and the holes and gaps made by them were filled by river sand. Shrubs were planted to help in soil conservation. To make the site more attractive and user-friendly, an open terrace with a low wall and less load was constructed in the slope. The pavement at the top of the slope was also replaced. Cording's report of February 1981 set out recommendations for establishing zones on the Swayambhu site where future development may take place; areas were also designated where no building activities should take place. Detailed information on all the sites, as well as 'Construction Zones' and 'No Construction Zones', is also provided in the report. The study revealed that most of the major historic structures have foundations that are sited away from the edge of slopes, or have been placed on rock that is not subject to sliding.

When this landslide crisis occurred, the Nepal government for the first time applied and enforced Article 3 of the Ancient Monument Preservation Act. The area was declared as a protected monument zone in 1978. Publication of this notification in Nepal Gazette helped to make it possible for the government to dismantle about nine houses that had developed cracks in the landslide.

According to Mr. Cording's recommendations, a Master Plan for the entire Swayambhu site was prepared in 1989 with financial support from German Technical Co-operation (GTZ). This is a very extensive Master Plan, the *Swayambhunath Conservation Master Plan* (also known as 'Swayambhu 2000'), was expected to free the area from illegal construction and encroachment by the year 2000. It provided a unique blend of objectives, as well as a vision: protection of the hill as a pilgrimage site with a tradition of well over 1500 years. It also deals with Swayambhunath as a living monument of Buddhist devotion and pilgrimage by defining a balance between growth and conservation. This Master Plan has given maximum consideration to the reports of the UNESCO experts. The Nepal government had declared the Swayambhu Conservation Programme as one of its priority programmes, and numerous repairs, restoration and infrastructure development activities have been carried out till recently. These have included constructing an open terrace at the rear of Shantipur, constructing toilets behind Karmaraja Mahavihar, extending the parking area, constructing a rest house at Manjusri Hill, flagstone paving of the courtyard of the Manjusri Temple, improving the stone stairway, re-afforestation of the entire hill, improving the supply and distribution of water, and last but not least the reconstruction of *Sabyagu baha*.

As mentioned above, the Swayambhu site was declared as a protected monument zone in late summer 1978, when it was threatened by heavy landslides. Then in August/September 1994, the earlier boundary of this protected monument zone was extended. When this site was included as one of the units of the World Heritage Site of Kathmandu Valley in 1979, many important monuments were included in it: Swayambhunath Stupa, Swayambhu Gumba, Singu Bahil, Harati Ajima temple, Shantipur, Karmaraj Gumba, Pratappur,

Anantapur, Maitri Gumba, Manjusri shrine, Dharmachakra Vihar, and Pulan Singu Stupa, among others.

The DOA has undertaken various follow-up activities as recommended by UNESCO experts to minimize the danger of land movement in the area since 1978–79. It has also taken many measures to improve the environment of this monument zone, receiving the full co-operation of the Department of Land Survey. Among the minor site improvement activities carried out by the DOA, the flagstone paving of many parts of the area is particularly noteworthy. The DOA has constructed open terraces in the southeastern slope after strengthening it against further possible danger of land movement. Similarly the DOA has built another open terrace in the northeastern corner in front of the Karmaraj Mahavihar after strengthening this area and providing sewerage facilities for drain water. The re-afforestation programme launched by the DOA was made possible thanks to assistance from the Germany GTZ organization.

In 1987, in connection with the third SAARC Summit Conference, many repair and infrastructure improvement activities were carried out in the Swayambhu Mahachaitya area. Flagstone paving was provided in the main courtyard. Numerous small votive *chaityas* were restored and around Shantipur paving stones were laid and a toilet was constructed to the west of the shrine. A *pati* (rest house) at Shantipur was restored, as were many votive stupas or chaityas at Manjusri. An old *hiti* (stone waterspout), *kuwa* (water hole), and a lotus pond at Buikhel were also restored at this time.

Today the Swayambhunath Conservation and Management Committee (Mahasamiti), established in July 1993, is responsible for conservation, development and maintenance activities in this monument zone. Since 1996/97 this Committee has been generating revenues through the entrance fees required of foreign tourists; it also receives some assistance from the government. Here, however, it should be noted that the Committee has been taking more of an interest in infrastructure development than in restoration, renovation, maintenance and cleaning activities. In 1999/2000, the DOA with the co-operation of the Mahasamiti carried out some minor repair works in the Mahachaitya and also renovated *Sabeygu Vihar* or *baha*. In the following year, the renovation of the temple of

Harati Mata was completed. The façade of an old house in the west of the Mahchaitya was changed and made more environment-friendly, and a small landslide problem behind the Gyanmala Prayer House was also controlled. In 2001/02 the Committee did some works in the area. It continued the afforestation programme, altered the façade of a house facing the Mahachaitya, renovated the Surya Binayak Ganesh temple, repaired the stone stairs, strengthened the area by constructing a retaining wall, and otherwise improved various infrastructures. In the next year, the Committee constructed a retaining wall to protect against land movement in the northwestern corner of the Saraswati Temple, reconstructed a long rest house (*lamo pati*) situated south of that temple and did stone paving in the courtyard. Further, it protected numerous sculptures by placing them in niches around the temple wall, changed the façade of a house nearby, and continued afforestation and other infrastructure development and maintaining activities as before (See Federation of Swayambhu Management and Conservation, BS 2059-60, BS 2060-61 and BS 2061-62, Audit Reports).

The construction of the so-called 'Shanti Pokhari' or 'Peace Pond' by the main entry point from the bus park, with a bronze statue of the Buddha, has been an eyesore to many people. Indeed, it should be seen as an unfortunate attempt of the Committee to construct a new artificial pond to replace a natural one. Moreover, Swayambhu receives enormous numbers of pilgrims and tourists every day, but its regular cleaning and maintenance is far from adequate.

But around the foot of the Swayambhunath hill, wealthy Tibetans as well as Buddhists from northern Nepal have been encroaching of late, constructing numerous parks with large statues of the Buddha and various lama gurus. To the right of the main entrance eastern gate, a big concrete statue of lama Chonghkama has been erected in a small park with a fishpond. Similarly in the western part of the foothills large statues of Guru Rimpoche (Padmasambhava) and Amitabha Buddha have been erected, in fact with the consent of the then Minister of Culture and other cabinet ministers of the time. Numerous such illegal constructions have taken place at the Swayambhu World Heritage Site under the protection of political leaders and ministers, without proper authority or permission from the concerned agencies including the DOA. It is highly debatable whether these new developments are worthy or amicable to the World Heritage Site?

In August 2003, the Pratappur Temple, one of the most important edifices of historical value built by King Pratap Malla 348 years ago and restored in 1921, was gutted by fire, and later completely destroyed by heavy monsoon rains. After some delay, the DOA dismantled the temple and reconstructed it completely, using traditional materials of brick powder *(surki)* and lime mortar instead of original mud mortar. In this reconstruction work, the DOA had the advantage of having a model from which to copy, because a similar type of temple, Anantapur, is located next to Pratappur. After performing *ksyama puja* to beg forgiveness in December 2003, the *jiba nyas puja* (ritual of removing the soul) was done and restoration work could start. It was completed within a year.

In 2003, 'Swayambhu Conservation Action Plan 2003' was prepared by John Sandey & Associates for Kathmandu Municipality, to improve and implement the laws to control encroachment. But as yet it has not been implemented.

The UNESCO/WHC/ICOMOS Missons were not happy with the prevailing situation at Swayambhu Mahachaitya, World Heritage Monument Zone. The UNESCO-ICOMOS-Government of Nepal Joint Mission in March/April 1998 was of opinion that there had been little success in resisting development pressures in the area immediately adjacent to the Ring Road, which passes to the north of Swayambhu. (Here we may mention such inappropriate new constructions as the police post at Buikhel, Karmaraj Mahvihar, and numerous other buildings constructed in the vicinity of the Ring Road.) On the other hand, the mission was pleased to note that no recent buildings of non-traditional design had been constructed near the stupa, and expressed their appreciation of the DOA's 1993 reconstruction of the Manjusri Sattal, which was done in traditional style and using traditional materials.

The Swayambhu Ghang Guthi trust owns almost the whole hill. It can sell, mortgage, lease and give tenancy right and permission to build a house, *gumba* or monastery to anyone in exchange for some revenue. Closer examination of land ownership patterns reveals that a vast area of the hill has been misused by this trust, for many years. As a result, many individuals as well as religious, educational and social organizations have registered a large portion of the territory in their own names. Those who own land on the hill and want to construct anything – a house, *gumba* or monastery – will simply ignore the authorities and the prescribed regulations and building codes. In many cases, they do not have even proper and valid documents for construction; those who have documents do not follow the norms prescribed by the government. Ultimately they construct houses, disguised as *gumbas* or monasteries or *mani* houses, destroying the façades of older buildings and sometimes demolishing them. In Swayambhunath Monument Zone there are 62 houses built against the norms prescribed by the DOA and more than 7 houses built without proper authorization.(reported in *Gorakhapatra* daily, 25 Chaitra BS 2058; also see Amatya, 1995, p. 12)

In sum: the Great Stupa of Swayambhu, a UNESCO World Heritage Site and the most prominent religious monument of the Kathmandu Valley, has been cared for throughout the centuries. The massive hill has now been stabilized and main historic structures on the site are no longer in jeopardy. However, severe encroachments continue, with the construction of inappropriate and disturbing new buildings.. Hawkers, curio vendors, stalls and refreshment shops further mar the aesthetic beauty, environment and religious atmosphere of the area. When will this, one of the world's most venerated Buddhist sites, proudly stand as the best maintained cultural heritage site in our country?

Swayambhunath stupa, around 1920

Swayambhunath stupa before renovation in 1918

Swayambhunath stupa

Swayambhunath: Aerial photograph, ca 1960 (courtesy: Ganesh Photo, Kathmandu)

Aerial photo of Swayambhu, from west

Aerial view of Swayambhu Hill after the landslide of August 1979

Checking and stabilizing the foundations of Anantapur Temple, 1980/81

General view of Swayambhu flanked by Pratappur and Anantapur

Reconstruction of Anantapur, 2004 (Courtesy: Department of Archaeology)

Anantapur after reconstruction, 2005

Samyagu Vihar, one of the vihars within the Swayambhu Monument Zone, after its recent renovation by the DOA

DOA repair of stone pavement around Swayambhu stupa

Repair of stone stairway within the Swayambhu Monument Zone, DOA

Director-General of UNESCO, Mr Rene Maheu, at Swayambhu, Shantipur, 1972

7

Conservation of Boudhanath (Khasa Chaitya) Monument Zone

> Wherever Buddhism has flourished, it has left its visible traces in the form of monuments, which have their origin in the tumuli of pre-historic times. These tumuli were massive structures in the forms of hemispheres, cones, pyramids, and similar plain, stereometrical bodies, which contained the remains of heroes, saints, kings or other great personalities.
>
> – Lama Anagarika Govinda, cited in Ehrhard, 1991

A stupa symbolizes the body of the Buddha, which is nothing other than the cosmos itself. The great stupa of Boudhanath is the principal centre of Tibetan Buddhist worship in the Kathmandu Valley – indeed, in the entire Indian sub-continent – and has long been a major destination of pilgrims from the Himalayas, Tibet and Southeast and East Asia. It is one of the largest and most significant Buddhist monuments in the world.

Concerning the origin of this stupa, there is one Tibetan and one Nepalese tradition. The Tibetan story is one of a poor but virtuous poultry-keeping woman. The Nepalese version connects it with the Lichchavi ruler King Manadev I (reigned ca AD 443–505) and a tale of patricide. According to this version, in order to end a devastating drought, the father of Manadev, King Dharmadev, engineered a strategy whereby the crown prince would unknowingly slay his own father. When Manadev realized the truth, he sought forgiveness, and eventually constructed the mammoth stupa of Boudhanath as penance, at a site located in what is today northeastern Kathmandu.

The *Gopalarajavamsavali* mentions that King Sivadeva I (ca AD 590–604) had the stupa restored. King Amsuverma (reigned ca 605–21) built houses around the stupa and beautified it. This tradition of restoration and renovation was continued during the ensuing Malla period as well. King Pratap Malla donated a *chattra* and, later, one Malimpa Lama donated a *gajura* in 1678. This latter occasion was graced by the presence of King Nirpendra Malla and his brothers. (H. Sakya, 1970.) But today there is no trace of the earlier Lichchavi elements in the vicinity of Boudhanath.

Though the stupa has become a major pilgrimage site of Tibetan Buddhists, its connection with Tibet developed clearly only in or around the 14th-century, when the renowned Tibetan sage Tongtang Gyelpo visited Boudha. According to another Tibetan tradition, over the centuries the stupa had become covered with dirt, sand and debris to the extent that it became invisible for many years. When the moment for realizing the prophecies of Guru Rinpoche (Padmasambhava) arrived, the holy reincarnation, the Yol-mo-pa Rig-'dzin Sakya bzan-po (Zanpo), unearthed the stupa, carried out repairs and restoration with extreme care, and made known its true worth. The name of the great stupa became once more as famous as that of the sun and the moon. This excavation and repair work took place during the second half of the 15th century and the first half of the 16th-century. During the excavation, the bones of the King Amsuverma were brought to light from the stupa's central axis (*yasti)* and were distributed to the people as blessings. Sakya Zanpo then reconstructed the stupa and probably enlarged the stupa, most likely giving it the form it has today. The finding of the bones of the Lichchavi king Amsuverma would indicate that the stupa was constructed as a votive monument after the death of this monarch. (Ehrhard, 1990.)

Since the 16th-century, the stupa has been intimately associated with the Tibetan tradition. Tenzin Norbu was the third reincarnation of Sakya Zampo. His successors, also known as Yolmo Tulkus, were appointed as the Tibetan government's residents at Boudhanath. It is believed that they undertook successive renovations to the fabric of the stupa. The Yolmo Tulkus were responsible for maintaining the stupa up to the 18th century. Under the Malla king Siva Simha (1587–1617) their function as 'sextons' was officially recognized, and a building to serve their needs was erected. (Ehrhard, 1991) In 1680 Rangrik Repa (Rang-rig ras-pa), a famous Kahgyu-Nyingma yogin from Spiti, consecrated his major work of restoring the stupa at Boudhanath. As mentioned in the previous chapter, he then offered 32 ounces of gold to King Parthivendra Malla with the request that it be used to finance the renovation of Swayambhu. (von Rospatt, 2001, p. 216).

Also other yogins engaged in the upkeep of the stupa at Boudhanath. Probably in 1728, the Tibetan holy man Rig-'dzin tshe-dbang norbu of Katok in eastern Tibet was commissioned to carry out repair activities by command of the ruler of South Tibet, Pho-lha-ba BSod-nams stobs-rgyas, who reigned from 1728 to 1747. In 1748 the Katok holy man and lama completed the renovation and consecration of the massive stupa at Boudha. (Ehrhard, 1989.)

In 1818/1819 the renowned Tibetan dzokchen yogin Shabkar Tsokdruk Rangdrol came to Kathmandu on pilgrimage. In 1821, with the permission of Nepal's Prime Minister Bhimsen Thapa, he had stupa's *harmika* steeple and spire covered with gilt copper sheets, and had a wall built around the stupa. Otherwise, not much change occurred during the 19th-century. In 1918/19 the Tibetan Lama Tokden Sakya Sri introduced various improvements (for example, the old wooden prayer wheels were replaced by copper ones), and this work was completed after his death in 1919 by his son Sonam Zangpo. Since 1919, little has changed at the stupa itself (Dowman, 1993).

As mentioned, Boudhanath is the principal centre of Tibetan Buddhism in the Kathmandu Valley and among the largest and most significant Buddhist monuments anywhere in the world. As it is a World Heritage Site and of international focus especially to many Buddhist nations, many people have taken an interest in the area. Unfortunately, however, most modern developments have been far from acceptable in conservation terms. The architectural and natural environment of this WHS have been totally ruined by the buildings that now surround the stupa, and the newly built two dozen *gumbas* of the various Tibetan Buddhist traditions. The rapid urbanization of the Kathmandu Valley, with a massive influx of newcomers, has had a tremendous impact on Boudhanath, causing crowding and pollution. It seems as if the local people, whenever they get the opportunity, tear down their old traditional houses and replace them with unsuitable box-type concrete buildings. The pace of such illegal construction has increased whenever there has been political turmoil in the country. Numerous such illegal buildings were erected during and after the Jana Andolan (Popular Revolt) I of 1998/98 and the recent Jana Andolan II of 2005/6.

Out of 88 buildings considered damaging to the stupa environs, 43 illegal buildings, constructed since 1984, need alteration. In 1998, it was found that at Boudhanath Monument Zone there are 45 houses built against the norms of prescribed by the DOA and 25 houses built without proper official documents (reported in *Gorakhapatra,* 25 Chaitra, BS 2058). One such structure, belonging to Mrs. Beti Laxmi Shakya, required total demolition prior to rebuilding according to an approved design. This case attracted international attention in 1997. Both UNESCO and the WHC vehemently opposed the illegal construction of this building and asked the DOA to take action to have it demolished immediately. In March 1998, a demolition team from the Nepal government with the help of the Kathmandu municipal authorities went into action and tore down the front façade and roof portion of the house. This action was perceived as a threat by the residents of Boudha, where there were so many other illegal buildings. The local people petitioned against this action, and made protests and processions with slogans against the DOA authorities. At one point they even surrounded the office of the DOA and burnt effigies of DOA authorities in front of the office building. In the end, however, the owner took advantage of weak administration, and built the house according to her own desire.

Even after Boudhanath had been declared a World Heritage Site, for many years the ward chairman and ward committee used to give permission to construct houses and to add floors after the original thatched roofs had been demolished. There are numerous examples where houseowners took no consideration whatsoever or did not at all heed the norms set by the DOA and simply built according to their own whims and fancies. (This is detailed, in Nepali, by S. Shrestha, 1989).

Development pressures are particularly acute at Boudhanath, and this has resulted in the loss of most of the historic structures that once surrounded the stupa. Of these, only a dozen houses or parts of houses now survive. Most of their replacements are of illegal height. The buffer zone defined in the World Heritage Site nomination forms was intended to protect the traditional setting of the historic stupa. However, all attempts to enforce this in practice have been almost entirely unsuccessful; the stupa is now quite engulfed by new buildings, which have spread out over what was once fertile farmland.

A great problem in keeping this WHS unspoiled and free from pollution is represented by the many *gumbas* (monasteries) that have mushroomed in the area. Until a few decades ago, Boudhanath was surrounded by a simple village of the Tamang people, and their farmland. Then, after the Dalai Lama escaped from Tibet, thousands of Tibetans fled to Nepal, and many of them found it natural to settle at Boudhanath. After all, the area was well known for its long-standing Tibetan traditions. Gradually the situation of Boudha began to change. Shelter had to be provided to the Tibetans; and to cater the various schools of Tibetan Buddhism, outsiders began donating to construct big *gumbas* in the vicinity of the famed stupa. Since the 1970s, more than two dozen large monasteries have been built in this area. They now dominate the whole environment, and have created problems for those who seek to maintain the norms of the Protected Monument Zone and the World Heritage Site of Boudhanath.

Restoration of Boudhanath Stupa in 1919/20 (Courtesy: Images of Nepal, p. 22)

Boudhanath from a distance from the west, before 1960

Boudhanath Stupa from the south, before 1960

Boudhanath Stupa

Boudhanath Stupa

Festival of lights at Boudhanath Stupa

8

Conservation of Monuments at Pashupatinath Monument Zone

Lord Pashupatinath – Shiva as the Lord of all living creatures – is the principal deity of Hindu Nepal. Pashupatinath Temple, on the banks of sacred Bagmati River in the Kathmandu Valley, is one of the earliest, most sacred and venerated holy pilgrim sites for Hindus from over the world. The main temple, which stands in the middle of the courtyard, has a square plan. It is two-tiered, built upon a plinth, and is 23.6 m. high. The four doors of the temple are silver and gilt-plated and richly decorated with painted images of deities. The two copper roofs are supported by numerous struts adorned with beautifully carved images of various Hindu gods and goddesses. The main image, the *mukhalingam,* is about one meter high and has faces in all four directions.

The temple of Lord Pashupatinath and its surrounding areas are not only of religious significance: they carry their own unique cultural, historical and archaeological identity. The main temple with its surrounding complex, together with a host of other temples and shrines, is a major religious focal point for millions of Hindus. Of course, in order to function as such an important religious site, the infrastructure must be in place. This includes the regular repair, maintenance and renovation of the hundreds of temples and other structures spread around the area.

An inscription at nearby Tilganga from AD 466 mentions the temple of Lord Vishnu Bikranta built by the Lichchavi king Manadev.

Another inscription, from 476, mentions the establishment of Ratneshwar Shivalinga during the reign of King Manadeva. These are only two few examples of the undoubted antiquity of this sacred site (D. Vajracharya, 1973, pp. 35, 50). An inscription of the famed King Amsuverma, from 625, provides further corroboration (Banerjee, 1980, p. 136). One legend tells the Pashupati temple was built by a king of the Somadeva dynasty in the 3rd century BC.

According to the most authentic and oldest surviving chronicle, *Gopalarajavamsavali*, written in the 13th century AD, it was the Lichchavi king Sri Supuspa Dev who constructed the temple of Sri Pashupati Bhattaraka. (Vajracarya & Malla, 1985, folio 19). This chronicle adds that another Lichchavi monarch, Sri Supuspa Verma, the grandfather of Manadev, beautified the temple of Pashupatinath (ibid, folio 20). The earliest inscriptional reference to conservation in the Pashupatinath Monument area dates from the time of the Lichchavi king Narendra Deva, in Sambat 103 (AD 679). A stone waterspout constructed in the vicinity of the temple was built during his reign and given to a *Vikshu Sangha* – a society of monks – for maintenance and care. An inscription dated Sambat 462 (AD 539) mentions that widow the Abhiri, after establishing the temple of Anuparameshwar Mahadev on the premises of the Pashupati temple, made arrangements for its repair and maintenance. According to an inscription of King Amsuverma at Deopatan dated Sambat 39 (AD 616), the temples of Ladita Mahadev, Surabhogesvara and Dakshinesvara were entrusted to the Adhasala Panchalika for maintenance (D. Vajracharya, 1973, p. 357, H. R. Joshi, BS 2030, p. 330). King Raghavadeva, during whose reign the Nepal Sambat or Nepal Calendar Era started (in AD 879), was also known as *Sri-Pashupati-bhattaraka-samvatsara*. This expression implies that the new era was started due to some religious event connected with the national shrine of Pashupatinath. Most probably some major constructions or restorations took place during this time inside the temple complex. Some historians are of the opinion that Gunakamadeva II, a king of the Thakuri dynasty, had the temple of Pashupatinath renovated and covered with a gilded copper roof. (Munakarmi, 1984, p. 84). King Sivadeva (AD 1099–1126) had completed the construction of temple of Pashupatinath and covered it with copper roof (Vajracarya & Malla, 1985, folio 24). According to some chronicles, King Sivadeva of the Thakuri dynasty had renovated the temple of Pashupatinath and made it three-storey structure (Munakarmi, 1984, p. 106). The chronicle *Gopalarajavamsavali* reports that in 1297 King Anantamalla Dev had the temple covered with a gilded roof; he also decorated the temple with the corner struts of four mythical animals and donated a gilded flag *(dhoja)*. At about the same time, Viramma Devi, the queen of King Jayaditya of Banepa, had the big bull of the main courtyard and the temple flagstaff covered with gilt-copper. (Vajracarya & Malla, 1985, folio 27.)

In AD 1349 the army of the Muslim invader Sultan Shumshud-din-Iliyas Ilias of Bengal destroyed the temple and broke the image of Pashupatinath into three pieces, as well as destroying numerous other monuments and sculptures of the Valley. Luciano Petech is of opinion that this invasion may have contributed, along with the perishability of the building material (timber), to the destruction of all the monuments of ancient Nepalese architecture, as none of the extant buildings in the Valley proper, however old the original foundations, seems to be earlier than the 15th-century (Petech, 1984, pp. 126–27).

The temple was restored and the image of Lord Pashupatinath was replaced in AD 1360 by Mahamantri Jayasimha Rama Vardhan. King Jayasthiti Malla Dev restored an old stone waterspout of Deo Patan (Jaya Bageswari) of the Pashupati area in memory of his queen Rajalla Devi (Vajracarya & Malla, 1985, folio 63).

It is clear that this temple and other monuments of this area have been repeatedly restored and conserved ever since Lichchavi times. According to Nepalese tradition, it is usually only after the reconstruction and renovation of a monument that some new things or decorative objects are added to the temple. At the Pashupati Temple, a stone slab inscription from AD 1413 notes that King Jyotir Malla, who was the son of Dharma Malla and the father of Yaksha Malla, erected a golden *kalasa* and flag serving jointly as the finial. Most probably it was after restoring the temple that the monarch offered this pinnacle. It is believed that the temple was thoroughly renovated and a new image of Lord Pashupatinath was reinstalled by King Jyotir Malla.

During the time of King Siva Simha Malla (AD 1578–1619) numerous repair and reconstruction activities were carried out in the

Pashupatinath area. His wife, Queen Ganga Rani, was a deeply religious person. She had the three-storey temple of Pashupatinath reconstructed, with two roofs. She also had the gilded pinnacle repaired, and paved the floor and the courtyard of the shrine with triangular bricks, some of which remain even today.

In 1697, during the reign of King Bhupalendra Malla, the woodwork of the Pashupati Temple had to be completely replaced, having been devoured by termites. This is recorded in a manuscript entitled *Guhyasiddi,* which describes the restoration work undertaken by the king in association with his mother, Riddhi Laxmi. The entire work took seven years to complete. Bhupalendra Malla also had numerous other important monuments in his kingdom restored.

According to a stone inscription dated NS 775 (AD 1655) at Pashupati, King Pratap Malla donated a golden finial to the temple of Pashupati. This would indicate that, after restoring the temple, Pratap Malla might have emplaced a new finial, most probably because the old one donated by King Jyotir Malla more than two centuries earlier had become damaged. Additionally, King Pratap Malla restored the temple of Sri Basuki in 1658, as shown by his gilded statues, along with images of his queens Rupamati and Ananta Priya, in the temple complex. In 1662, King Pratap Malla built the shrine of Guheswari.

During the reign of King Nirpendra Malla (1674–80), a nobleman named Sikhawla had all four doors and tympanums of the Pashupati Temple covered with gilt. A chronicle also mentions that during the reign of Nirpendra Malla, a Maithali Brahman had murdered one of his own relatives; as a penalty, his property was confiscated and the money was used to restore the main temple at Pashupatinath, to establish an image of Daksinamurti, and to repair the Bhubaneswari Temple in the Pashupatinath complex (Koirala, BS 2051, p. 374).

In the early 19th-century, Prime Minister Bhimsen Thapa had four inner doors and four outer doors covered with silver; the silverwork of the southern gate of the temple is also attributed to him. According to inscription of the tympanum of the southern gate dated BS 1875 (AD 1818) Prime Minister Bhimsen Thapa had the door covered with silver; later on his brother, Ranabir Singh Thapa, had it gilded.

The Pashupatinath Monument Zone received considerable attention during the oligarchic rule of the Rana Prime Ministers (1846–1950). The founder of the Rana oligarchy, Prime Minister Jung Bahadur Rana, carried out extensive repairs of the steps of Aryaghat leading to the Guhyesvari Temple through Mirgasthali, which had been constructed by his father Ram Krishna Kuwar in 1774, and the resting places for those brought to this place on the eve of their death. Ram Krishna Kuwar had also left a trust or *guthi* of 263 *ropanis* of land for the maintenance of the steps.

Guheswari is the second most revered shrine at Pashupatinath. In 1866, Prime Minister Jung Bahadur Rana dismantled the old boundary wall of the temple and constructed a new broad one. He also had the Kunda Bhairav covered with golden sheet decorated with *navratna,* nine different precious stones. In 1908, repair works to this shrine were done under Prime Minister Chandra Shumsher. He had the floor of the inner sanctuary paved with tiles from Britain, and repaired the Kalash Bhairav by adding more gold. After the earthquake of 1934, Prime Minister Juddha Shumsher renovated the *sattal*.

Also after the restoration of the monarchy in Nepal, attention continued to be given to Pashupatinath. In 1959, King Mahendra had various improvement works carried out in the temple complex (Regmi, 1969, p. 73). In 1997, Mr. Daya Ram Mathema donated approximately Rs. 300,000 to the Pashupati Area Development Trust for repair of the silverworks of six arches, three in the south and three in the east, on the prayer chambers built around the inner sanctuary of the Guheswari temple. These arches had originally been donated by his grandfather, Sardar Hari Bhakta Mathema, and his uncle, Kaji Bhagwat Bhakta Mathema. As recently as in 2003/04, a major renovation of the Guheswari temple was undertaken by the Pashupati Area Development Trust. All old and rotten wooden structures and artifacts were then replaced by new ones.

When speaking of the conservation of monuments in Nepal we should not forget that, in order to conserve, stabilize and strengthen these edifices, the roofs, walls, floors and other parts of the structure and architecture are frequently repaired and restored using new materials; likewise, woodworks are often covered with silver and gilt. For example, the doors and woodworks of the temple were covered with ornamental silverwork variously during the times of Rana Bahadur Shah and Griwan Yuddha Bikram Shah. In 1814, the daughter of King Rana Bahadur Shah and the eldest sister of King Griwan Yuddha, Princess Bilaswati, had the tympanum of the eastern gate of the main temple decorated with gilded silver works. Some two years earlier, the priest Raghav Ballav Aryal had the southern gate of the main temple covered with gilded silver works. And in 1814, General Amar Singh Thapa had the northern inner main gate of the temple covered with gilded silver works. In 1834, during the reign of King Rajendra Bikram Shah, an influential official named Kulananda Jha had the main doors of the west, north and eastern directions of the temple covered by silver works, and also built a large rest house in the west of the courtyard. In those days it was customary for influential families to receive permission to restore, renovate, decorate and silver-cover the woodwork and architectural fixtures of monuments. Prime Minister Ranoddip Singh (1877-1885) had the floor of the temple of Pashupatinath paved with white marble slabs.

In 1889, during the time of Prime Minister Bir Shumsher, Kaji Bhagwat Bhakta Mathema, son of Sardar Hari Bhakta Mathema, had all 552 lion-faced wooden cornices of the Pashupati temple silver-covered. In 1925, Prime Minister Chandra Shumsher repaired the gilded copper roofs that had covered the temple of Pashupatinath from the days of King Nirpendra Malla. It was at this time that the woodwork was painted in bright colours as a decorative-cum-protective measure. Large-scale renovation of the temple was thus carried out within living memory by Prime Minister Chandra Shumsher in the early 20th century.

As noted, *guthis* have been established for the conservation, restoration and maintenance of monuments in Nepal since the time of the Lichchavi rulers. In the case of Pashupatinath, an agency known as 'Amali' was responsible for the maintenance of monuments in this area since 1796. With the support of the people, the Amali would undertake repair works if the *ghats* or bathing places on the riverbanks had become damaged. During the Shah period in the 19th century, forced labour was also occasionally used for maintenance and repair works of Pashupatinath temple and the temple of Basuki: the chief priest was empowered to arrange this.

In 1904, Pashupatigosora, an office responsible for maintenance, repair and development of all types of edifices of the Pashupatinath area, was established. This body was made responsible for carrying out minor repairs of monuments at Pashupati and Guheswari, and was also given responsibility for those monuments which had no *guthi* support. It was allowed to carry out, independently, repair works costing up to fifty rupees – a not inconsiderable sum at the time. If more money was needed, Pashupatigosora had to get approval from the office of the Public Works Department. The materials needed for repairs were readily made available from various districts.

Inside the Pashupati area, no structures were to be built without the permission of Pashupatigosora and the Bada Guruju (chief priest). Until the formation of Pashupati Area Development Committee *(Pashupatichetra Sudhar Thatha Bikas Samiti)* in 1977, Pashupatigosora also dealt with these activities. In fact, for some time even after the establishment of the PADC, duplication of work in maintenance and repair activities continued.

During the reign of King Mahendra (1955–72) numerous repair and construction activities were carried out by *Upatyakanchal Tatkalin Sudhar Samiti* in the name of the conservation and development of Pashupati area, but they were not done in accordance with archaeological principles. For example: inside the main courtyard of the temple many new concrete structures were built. The big rest house known as 'Mahendrasahara' above the main western gate was constructed; all small temples and structures were plastered with cement and painted, and numerous small shivalingas and sculptures were removed. On the other hand, the restorations of Mukti Mandap, the Basuki Temple and the Kotilingeshwar Temple, as well as the flagstone paving of the main courtyard, were carried out in somewhat acceptable manner.

During the time of the late King Mahendra, the courtyard of the Guheshawari Temple was paved with flagstones, and the rest houses around the temple were restored and renovated. Here also the main gateway in the north was constructed – unfortunately, with cement. The temple courtyard of Bankali was paved with flagstones, boundary walls were constructed and the rest house was restored. The temple of Gorakhanath, at Bankali, was also restored. At nearby

Chabahil, the tile roof of the temple of Chandra Vinayak was removed and replaced by copper roofing. The struts were also repaired and changed. The rest house in the west of the temple was repaired. The stone spout known as 'Ganga Hiti' in the north of the temple was restored. In the area from the east of Gauri Ghat Bridge and to the west, *ghats* were constructed and paved with stone. At Kirateyshor Temple, the landslide problem was controlled by constructing protective walls on the right and left sides of the main road in the northern direction. All these activities made the Pashupati area somewhat more attractive and open – but no lovers of art and architecture can commend the liberal use of cement and the haphazard application of red colour at that time in the monuments of the Valley.

In 1977, as mentioned, the PADC was established, under the chairmanship of Sardar Bhupal Man Singh. However, little was achieved in the field of monument restoration and conservation. Then in 1981, Mr. Ramesh Jung Thapa was appointed the new chairman of this committee. As the former Director-General of the Department of Archaeology, he had some experience of monument restoration activities. And indeed, during his tenure of office several important restoration and conservation activities were carried out in the monument zone. The residences of chief priest and another priest were restored. However, the ancient Malla architecture of these houses was not kept intact, and many new elements were introduced. The eastern wing of Shankaracharya Math was restored. The rest houses of the eastern and northern sides of Jitjung Prakashewar temple were also restored, and the rest house of Bhakun Tole was repaired. But more attention was given to new constructions than to conserving and preserving old structures and monuments. In the rest house by the northern side of Jitjung Prakashewar temple there had been attractive wall paintings of Gorkhanath in various *yogasan,* but during repair they were neglected and thus lost. The architecture of Amalkot house was totally changed – and so on.

The Ancient Monument Preservation Act (AMPA) of 1956 has given protection to this monument zone, but the temple complex is also protected by a separate piece of legislation – the Pashupati Area Development Trust Act of 1987. In 1982, Pashupatinath Monument

Zone was declared as protected monument zone (PMZ) according to the fifth amendment of the AMPA.

A separate executive committee has also been established under the Trust, to conduct and supervise various development and conservation activities within the zone, where there are some 495monuments of varying size. A Master Plan for its conservation and development was launched in 1990/91. Initially, the DOA assisted the Trust in its repair and conservation activities. As a line agency, the DOA restored some important monuments of this area during the 1980s: prominent among them were the temples of Gurudakshina Murti and Tamreshwar Mahadev Mandir.

The Pashupatinath Monument Zone was inscribed as one component of the Kathmandu Valley World Heritage Sites (KVWHS) in 1979. At that time, the ancient Newa settlement of Pashupati Deopatan and Mirgasthali forest, with the sanctuaries of Guhyesvari, Visvarupa and Gorakhnath, were included in the inscription, whereas the Gauri Ghat area was omitted. Then in 1998, on recommendation of the visiting UNESCO/ICOMOS Mission, Gauri Ghat and the *hitis* opposite the Rajarajesvari Temple and the 15-m. stretch across the Bagmati River were included in the re-defined boundary zone of Pashupatinath Monument Zone. Thus, the World Heritage Site now includes such major monuments as the temples of Pashupati and Vasuki, Arya Ghat, Bachhareshwari, Rajrajeshwari, Panchadeval, Banakali, Jayabageshwari, Bhunaneshwari, Dakshinamurti, Gauri Ghat, Vishwarup, Goraknath, Guyeshwari, and others.

In 1988, under the chairpersonship of Her Majesty Queen Pashupati Kshetra Bikas Kosh, the Pashupati Area Development Trust (PADT) was formed, and a separate independent legal status was given to it. This trust constituted an authority that was to ensure the preservation of the site as well as to guide its further development. In 1994, some important changes were introduced in the organization of this trust, and the Minister of Culture was made co-chairperson. Since that time, the PADT has become all-powerful in this area. Each year, selected restoration and conservation activities are undertaken. With the objective of protection, the PADT has already classified all monuments of this area in accordance with the Ancient Monument Preservation Act. To facilitate conservation work, the Zone was divided into sixteen different areas, containing some 492 monuments.

In 1994, a building code *(Mapdanda)* for the Pashupati area was published and promulgated. According to this code, any new buildings should be constructed in traditional Nepalese architectural style, and with a maximum height of 35ft inside the monument zone. Demolition of old houses would be permissible only after obtaining necessary permission from the trust. Before any new construction or repair of old houses in the area could commence, maps and plans should be submitted and permission obtained. On the whole, the new building code seemed acceptable. In practice, however, the trust could not efficiently implement it in many cases, and many ugly cement structures soon sprouted up.

For the protection and development of the built environment of Pashupatinath Monument Zone, a Master Plan was made ready in 1988. But even one decade later, nothing much had been achieved. Then in 1998 the Ten-Year Master Plan was updated. This proved to be a very ambitious document that envisaged spending about Nepalese rupees two billion, six million and three hundred thousand Nepali rupees (2 *araba*, 6 *crore*, 30 *lakh*). The aim of the Master Plan is to give life to the religious environment of Pashupati area, through the purification of the Bagmati River, the protection and preservation of religious, archaeological and social edifices, and the development of infrastructures. The Master Plan divides the Pashupati Monument Zone into three main areas: core area, consonant area and continuum area. But this Master Plan was not put into action until 2001. It has now been decided to devote substantially less –approximately 13 hundred million (13 *crore*) Nepalese rupees – to monument restoration activities.

The PADT did some commendable restoration work inside the monument area. Up until 1994, several important monuments had been restored and repaired by this trust. These include the temples of Daksinamurti, Tamreshwar Mahadev and Chandra Binayak, stone spouts like Barun Dhara, Arun Hiti and Baha Hiti, the *ghat* in the south of Ramghat, reconstruction of the dam at Rajrajeshswori, the restoration of the 19th century Biswarupa temple, Nirvaneshore, as well as other activities.

Inside the main courtyard, however, the reconstruction of the Unmanta Bhairav Temple by the southern gate of the main shrine stands as a poor example of renovation. This temple was constructed by King Jayasthiti Malla in the 14th century. Unfortunately, today it is totally covered with glittering brown tiles, not at all suited to the environment of the temple complex. To reconstruct the Bhairav Temple, in such fashion, in front of the beautiful and mighty Pashupati temple must be seen as an unwise decision on the part of the authorities responsible. This huge cement structure, covered with glittering coloured tiles, is surely one of the worst examples of recent conservation activity in the entire country.

In January 2004, the PADT began restoration of the Sadavarta Sattal (Pashupati Mahashana Ghar) – where once each month the main feast (*Maha Bhoja* or *Mah Shana*) offered to the Lord Pashupati on the full moon night is prepared. One of the major monuments of the Shah period, it is a large three-storey courtyard building constructed of *dachi appa* bricks with high-quality carved timber decoration. At the same time the trust also commenced the restoration of another important building, the Saptami Shardha Ghar, where the death anniversary ritual is performed on the seventh day of the dark moon fortnight each month. The intention had been to complete these works by 2007, but only 50% of the restoration has been accomplished as of this writing. The PADT has also been restoring the south wing of Pancha Dewal *dharamsala* or rest house. The west range of this courtyard has been recently reconstructed to a good standard, using lime-*surkhi* mortar. The east range, where the posts of the external *dalan* were extruding through the pine lintels, has recently been repaired *in situ.* These *dharamsalas* are used as a home for needy elderly people who have no family support. The PADT is also restoring some *patis* (rest houses) by the southern gate and elsewhere, and carrying out maintenance work in the core area. Further, it has been involved in constructing the *ghat* at Rajrajeshawri, roof repairing of Jitjung Prakashewar Sattal, and repairing walls in the Guheshwari area.

For effective implementation of the Master Plan and to make the core area pollution-free, spacious and functional, in 2002 the PADT decided to demolish nearly 120 houses or structures in the area. As in other monument zones and WHS of the Kathmandu Valley, also in

Pashupati MZ the pressure of urbanization has become tremendous, with encroachment in public lands, open spaces, and socio-religious structures like *sattals, patis, pauwas* (roadside shelters) and other monuments increasing day by day, making it necessary to demolish these illegal structures.

Under the first phase of the Master Plan programme, the PADT removed the unauthorized persons living in the various *patis* and *sattals*. In all, 110 illegal houses in the core areas of the temple complex were demolished, and satisfactory compensation was provided to the owners. The PADT demolished all houses in the west of the main entrance gate except those with historic connections. Local people who had commercial interests and had been running various types of shops in the area brought this action to court. The PADT argued that these houses were built only after 1943: before then, there had been no such houses except some *sattals* and *patis*. Almost all these houses were built without permission and were thus illegal. Some owners protested against the demolition order, maintaining that these houses have direct relationship with the temple and the various religious-cultural functions held there. In the end, the court dismissed the case, ruling in favour of the PADT.

Here it should be noted that, although the PADT has attempted to make Pashupatinath, the holiest site of the country, more open and more presentable, in some cases they have acted in haste. First of all, they should have documented each and every house in detail, specifying its history, function, current use, legality and so on. They should never forget that Pashupatinath and the cultural heritage of the site belong primarily to the local residents, and only secondarily to others. The PADT's decision to move the local people who were directly connected to the various rituals and festivals connected with the temple at the site known as Uma-Kunda might be correct, but some of the structures that were demolished were in fact of great importance to the local inhabitants. One example is the houses of the Bhandaris, where they claimed to have had their family shrine for generations. Whether it is better for the country that the Pashupatinath Monument Zone should exist without local people living within its precincts is a very delicate and disputable question. Only the future will tell. It is true that this demolition step made this area cleaner and more open. The PADT has also retained some very important structures and houses of historic and ritualistic value. But it should never forget the necessity of ensuring the smooth running of the entire regular festivals and rituals conducted in the zone. This is the ancient cultural heritage of all the people and of the sacred shrine. The PADT should guarantee that the Master Plan is implemented so as to work for preservation of cultural heritage of the area, not to destroy or diminish it.

In the Pashupatinath Monument Zone there were, as of 1998, three houses built against DOA norms, and twelve that had been constructed without approved drawings (reported in *Gorakhapatra,* 25 Chaitra, BS 2058). The UNESCO/ICOMOS mission recommended that these traditional houses of the core area should not be demolished but retained and used, after necessary repairs. They held that the demolition of historic fabric should be stopped, and the Master Plan elaborated or amended accordingly. In my view, however, the Mission had not undertaken serious study or research, but merely sought cheap public sympathy and support. At any rate, all agreed that the PADT should not take such drastic demolition action in haste and should be always guided by rational considerations. We should support the PADT in its attempts to make this core area more open, spacious and functional – but we should also warn it to exercise care not to demolish any structure before ascertaining its role in the cultural context. How far the actions and judgement of the trust could save and preserve the cultural heritage of this area remains to be seen.

In the vicinity of Pashupati Monument Zone stands a very ancient stupa known as Dandeo Chaitya or Charumati Vihar, the Chabahil Stupa. Findings of Kushan coins and numerous other Lichchavi coins and inscribed antiquities have proved that the stupa certainly dates from the Lichchavi period. It was probably built in the beginning of the Christian era, perhaps even earlier. (In fact, one local tradition holds that Chabahil was originally established by the daughter of the great Mauryan emperor Ashoka, who ruled in the 3rd century BC.)

It seems that the stupa was renovated at the time of King Pratap Malla in 1653–56 (Rajbamsi, 1970, pp. 76, 82) During the late Malla period, at the time of King Mahindra Singh Dev, a member of the Chitrakar family (artists' clan) from Deo Patan restored the images of the Five Buddhas in 1715 and presented a gilded pinnacle to the stupa. Repairs were also undertaken in 1845, during the reign of King Rajendra Bikram Shah, when the central pole *(yasti)* was broken. Members of the Sakya clan of Deo Patan area did the actual restoration work. To insert the new *yasti,* the dome or *garbha* was opened, and many figures of different Buddhist deities were found. (Oldfield, 1880/1974, pp. 258–59). Recently the Chabihil Stupa was renovated in 2002, when cracks had developed in the *harmika* after heavy rainfall that year. Inspection revealed that unless renovation was undertaken immediately, the *haramika* might fall at any time. A detailed description (in Nepali) of these renovation activities is given in Darnal, 2005.

Pashupati Arya Ghat before 1934

Panchayan Shiva Temples, Pashupati

Cleaning of Pashupati Temple in 2003 (Courtesy: Department of Archaeology)

Pashupati Temple from the east

Panoramic view of Pashupati Monument Area during cleaning in 2003

Panoramic view of Pashupati area

9

Conservation of Changu Narayan World Heritage Site

The Changu Narayan temple site, dating back to the Lichchavi period, is believed to be one of the Valley's earliest settlements. Until recently, the pillar inscription of King Manadev, dated BS 521 (AD 464) and situated in the temple precincts, was one of the oldest evidences of recorded history of Nepal. Architecturally the temple of Changu Narayan is probably the earliest surviving example of Nepalese traditional temple architecture. In ancient times, this area, situated to the east of Kathmandu near Bhaktapur, was known as Doladri, Charu Giri, Champak Giri and Kileshwar Giri. With its hillside location, it also served as a fortress. Chronicles relate that Changu Narayan was established by King Hari Dutta Verma in AD 325. The AD 464 pillar inscription of King Manadev also corroborates that a temple had existed on the site before the pillar was erected. However, according to an ancient chronicle found by Cecil Bendal in the Durbar Library (the National Archives of Nepal) dated NS 177 (AD 1057), it was King Visnugupta (AD 633) who founded Changu Narayan (Petech, 1984, p. 6).

The temple area has many excellent examples of Lichchavi sculpture, including the 7th-c. Biakuntha Narayan as well as the Garudashana Vishnu, the Vishnu Biswa Roop and the Tri-Bikram, all from the 8th-century. Otherwise, it is especially famed for its remarkable woodcarvings. The entire temple area can be considered as an open-air treasure house or museum of arts and architecture.

Revered by both Hindus and Buddhists, Changu Narayan has been the most important site for worshippers of the Lord Vishnu since early times. To Nepalese Buddhists, it is seen as the shrine of the god Hari Hari Hari Bahana Lokeshwar. Moreover, it is one of the few sites from the mediaeval period which has survived the ravages of time. In addition to the temple, the Changu Narayan area includes several smaller shrines, among them the Kileshwar Temple, the Chinnamasta Temple, Laxmi Narayan, Kanti Bhairav and others.

The history of conservation at Changu Narayan dates back at least 1500 years, to the Lichchavi period. When King Manadev erected the pillar inscription in AD 464, the temple was already about one hundred years old. Nepalese temples, built mainly of wood, bricks and mud mortar, cannot survive more than a century, so it seems clear that King Manadev must have carried out either restoration or renovation works at Changu Narayan. In the 7th century, King Amsuverma repaired the Garuda Narayan, the main idol of the temple. As this was nearly 150 years after Mandev's rule, also he must have either restored or repaired the temple. The inscription left by him enumerates the rules and regulations that he prescribed for the maintenance and strengthening of the fortress at Changu Narayan.

After that time, we have records only after a gap of about five hundred years, when King Simha Dev (1099–1122) had the temple restored, but it seems likely that repairs or renovations had been carried out on various earlier occasions as well. According to the chronicle *Gopalarajavamsavali,* after King Simha Dev, Queen Viramma Devi had the temple restored. (D Vajracharya & Malla, 1985, folio 27). In 1508, a great earthquake shook the Valley, damaging the temple of Changu Narayan. It was later repaired by Princess Devaki Devi, the granddaughter of King Raya Malla.

Another chronicle mentions the renovation carried out by King Bishva Malla of Bhaktapur (1548–60) from the very foundations. The temple was again restored during the reign of King Shiva Simha Dev, by his consort Queen Ganga Rani, in 1585.

The Changu Narayan temple complex was equally venerated during the Malla period, and was restored and renovated on numerous occasions. During the reign of King Nirpendra Malla, the temple of Kileshwar was constructed by two brothers, Khar Man

Singh Bharo and Giridhar. They also had the temple of Chhinamasta Devi decorated with carved struts. In 1691, King Bhupalendra Malla had the temple of Kileshwar restored. Three years later, together with Queen Mother Riddhi Laxmi, he had the Changu Narayan Temple restored and offered a gilded tympanum. In 1702 the temple was gutted by fire. Only two years later, the widow of Bhupalendra Malla, Bhuwan Laxmi, had it completely renovated, and also erected a golden statue of her husband in front of the temple. Five years later, she had the uppermost roof of the temple constructed of gilt copper. What we see today is the temple as it must have stood in 1709 (Pruscha, 1975, pp. 156–57).

In Rana times, the wife of Prime Minister Ranaudip Singh, Queen Hari Priya Devi, had the Chaugera Sattal (rest house) constructed in 1879. Most probably, portions of the temple were repaired at that time, and outside the temple courtyard, two rest houses – Inbaha Sattal and Bhimsen Pati – were also renovated. After the earthquake of 1934, Prime Minister Juddha Shumsher renovated the Chaugera Sattal. On this occasion the traditional tile roofs were replaced with corrugated metal sheets. In 1975, King Mahendra renovated the top gilded copper roof and also the lower tile roofs of the temple and made it presentable. However, during this renovation the finely carved struts were covered by inappropriate, non-traditional colours (Khanal, 1983, pp. 22–59.)

In 1977, the Master Plan for the Conservation of the Cultural Heritage in the Kathmandu Valley was prepared and presented to the Nepal government for implementation by UNESCO. The Master Plan recommends improving the approach road from Bhaktapur, and suggests reforestation of the whole hill. All corrugated metal roofs around the courtyard should be replaced with tiled roofing. The Plan also notes that the roofs of the main temple and the temples of Laxmi Narayan and Shiva in the southwest corner of the complex need repair and consolidation. Additional site improvement and consolidation activities are also suggested.

On the call of UNESCO for the protection and development of Changu Narayan Monument Zone in 1985, a team of architects and graphic designers from Sydney School of TAFE and Randwick School of TAFE in Australia conducted architectural survey and research and survey of the site. They then prepared detailed documentation, with drawings, photographs and video-films. In 1986, the TAFE colleges also organized a promotional exhibition of the Changu Narayan site in Sydney.

The Changu Narayan Temple Site was declared a Protected Monument Zone in 1984, and is also included as one of the elements comprising the Kathmandu Valley World Heritage Site. Among the major monuments included in the World Heritage List are the following: Changu Narayan Temple, Krishna Shrine, Nriteshwar Shrine, Narayan (Vishnu) Platform, Mahavishnu Platform, Shiva (Mahadev) Shrine, Avalokiteshwar Platform, Ganesh Shrine, Chhinna Masta Temple, Mahdev Shrine, Vishrarupa Platform, Laxmi-Narayan Temple, Bhairav Shrine and Kileshwar Mahadev Temple.

In 1988, the Nepal government set up a team under the chairmanship of this author, who was then Director-General of the Department of Archaeology, to prepare a Master Plan for the overall development and protection of the Changu Narayan site. This Master Plan identifies 42 major and minor monuments to be repaired and restored. Apart from the restoration activities, approach roads and walkways are to be repaired and maintained, an afforestation programme launched, and picnic spots and parks developed. Moreover, the living conditions of the local people are to be improved by providing sanitation, drinking water and sewerage and facilities. This Master Plan is intended not only to save one of our most precious cultural heritage sites but also to encourage tourism.

The 1988 Master Plan recommends the restoration of twelve temples, ten shrines, two rest houses, four sattal rest houses, seven stone waterspouts, one pond, four courtyards, one priestly residence and one open platform, and the paving of about 2500 square meters of area. The conservation and improvement of the forest and other infrastructures are also recommended. The monument site is situated on a small hillock, so the possibility of landslides should not be discounted. Therefore is it proposed to establish geodetic points, in order to monitor hill movement. For implementation purposes, the Master Plan divides the Changu Narayan Monument Zone into three parts: core area, inner area and outer area. A five-year implementation plan has been drafted to fulfil the aims and objectives of the Master Plan.

Since 1987, considerable repair and restoration activities have been undertaken at Changu Narayan WHS as a follow-up to the implementation of the UNESCO Master Plan and the above-mentioned Master Plan prepared by officials of the Nepal government. The platforms of Mahavishnu and Lokeshwar have been repaired, and protection has been provided for sculptures. Repairs have been carried out on the tile roof of the eastern side of the main temple, which was badly overgrown with vegetation and was leaking. Herbicides were used to stop further plant growth. The plinth of the image of Vishnu Vishwaroop has been improved and protected by providing a brick arch for shade. The 17th-century roofs of the temple of Kileshwar have been repaired, and herbicides applied to prevent the growth of vegetation in the future. The temple struts with Asta Bhairavs were protected by using the insecticide zelophin.

The Changu Narayan is a typical example of a Newa village from the mediaeval period. It is characterized by small *jingiti* tile roofed houses on both sides of the narrow serpentine road that leads to the courtyard of the main temple, situated on the west side of the village. In the village itself, the Ganesh Temple was entirely demolished and reconstructed in replica. In 1988, repairs were carried out on the two-storey *sattal* facing the Ganesh Temple across the village street as well as the L-shaped Bhimsen Pati near the eastern gateway of the temple. The corrugated roof of this *pati* was replaced with traditional tiles; the outer walls were repaired with *dachi appa,* and the floor was paved with *teliya* bricks. Sewerage on both sides of the rest house was also repaired. The sculptures of Surya, Ardha-Narieshwar, Uma-Maheshwar, Laxmi-Narayan and other deities were re-installed in their original places. The earlier bad repair of the Laxmi-Narayan Temple was to some extent improved. The temple plinths were repaired with *dachi appa,* and the 8th-century sculptures of Vishnu-Bikranta and Narasimha belonged were provided with arched brick shelters. The *Inbaha Hiti* (stone waterspout) and the rest house behind it were restored to their original forms. But the complete restoration of the Laxmi-Narayan Temple was planned for the future.

However, in 1990/91, acting on orders from the Royal Palace, the Nepal government established a committee, *Kathmandu Upatyaka Samskritik Thatha Dharmik Chetra Bikas Samanoya Samiti* (the Kathmandu Valley Cultural and Religious Sites Development and

Co-ordination Committee), and the WHS of Changu Narayan was put under its umbrella. Even after the formation of this committee, the DOA continued its repair and other development activities at Changu Narayan for some years. Thereafter, for several years, this new Committee undertook various construction works in the Changu Narayan area which did not at all comply with any archaeological principles. To cite only one example of bad restoration practice: the old *pokhari* (pond) at the entrance to the village was renovated in a different form, using newly quarried stone and cement mortar.

During the 6th and 7th Five-Year Plan period, restoration and infrastructure development activities continued at Changu Narayan WHS. In 1997, numerous small shrines and sculptures were protected and restored; moreover, with support from the UNDP Quality Tourism Project, the Bhajan Pati (Sanga Fah) was restored for the benefit of the local people as a venue for traditional musical functions. In the next year, the Laxmi-Narayan temple of the courtyard was restored, and the repair of the walls and plinths of the Chaugera Sattal of the main courtyard commenced. In 1999, the temple of Chandi Bhairav was restored, thanks not least to the involvement of the local people. The main courtyard of the temple was paved with triangular bricks made in the original design and size, and the old staircase was repaired. In that same year, a small shrine to the goddess Saraswati was also repaired.

In 2000, about 225 meters of the roof and the pinnacle of the main temple were repaired and restored. In the following year the uppermost roof of the temple was completely restored, and restoration of the Amatya Sattal began. In 2002, the stone stairway of Changu Narayan was repaired, and restoration of the roofs of the main temple was completed. In the following year, work on restoring the Amatya Sattal was completed. This authentic restoration was possible with the help of an old painting by Kaji Man Karmacharya, made available to the DOA by the courtesy of Sukra Sagar Shrestha, a retired DOA archaeologist. The DOA is preparing to open a site museum in this building.

As mentioned above, the DOA has recently restored one of the rest houses, the Amatya Sattal on the southern side of the courtyard. This renovation did not change the traditional appearance of the 300-year-old *sattal*. Traditionally the temple complex had been maintained by a local *guthi*, which had income from the land donated to it. But, after the establishment of the Guthi Undertakings, income and responsibility for maintaining the temple complex was shifted to this new organization. Since that time, due to poor administration of this organization, all-important monuments of the Valley have been suffering – including Changu Narayan. Timely rescue measures are not enacted, and once a monument is badly damaged it always has to wait for the DOA to come to the rescue. Recently the DOA has also completed renovation of one ancient stone waterspouts called Narayan Hiti.

In 1998, the recently established Kathmandu University was preparing to construct university buildings at Changu Narayan WHS. When this came to the notice of the DOA, this author, as Acting Director-General, went to inspect the construction site. The university had already laid the foundation stone of one of the main buildings on a small hilltop on the eastern side of the main hill – an area within the buffer zone of the Changu Narayan WHS. In this area the university had acquired about 40 or 50 *ropanis* of land, and local enthusiasts had promised more lands in future if needed. At the construction site, some 50,000 bricks had also been dumped. Dr. Suresh Raj Sharma, chief promoter of the university, who was also one of my senior colleagues in the Ministry of Education, repeatedly tried to convince me to grant permission for the construction works. I requested Dr. Sharma to show me the engineering and architectural blueprints of all the buildings under construction. He showed me five or six blueprints, of buildings planned for construction during the first phase. Although most of the buildings would be constructed in the buffer zone of the WHS, and not within the core monument zone, I felt that an ever-expanding institution like this university project was not at all feasible on that site. I also felt that local politics strongly supported the project without knowing its future consequences. The Education Secretary and Ministers were also in a very tricky situation. It would be difficult for them to say no to Dr. Sharma, who had always been a very pleasant and efficient colleague in the Ministry; but neither could they force the DOA, which was responsible for protecting the WHS, to grant permission.

As my own relations with Dr. Sharma had always been very agreeable and co-operative, I wanted to help him and if possible to settle this problem amicably. Keeping these things in mind I paid numerous visits to the site, but found that I could not venture to contravene and destroy the norms and conditions of the World Heritage Convention. Moreover, once the university was established there, the forest area around the WHS and the small mediaeval-type village would soon be destroyed. Thus, both the natural and the cultural heritages would be threatened. Again and again the issue was discussed in the Ministry, but no one could come up with a solution. In particular, one vested interest group was highly critical to my reservations. When I realized that merely talking in the office would never help to solve the problem, I requested the Minister as well as the Assistant Minister and the Secretary to visit the site and discuss the issue on the spot. Taking with us all relevant documents, we went to the site. There we could agree that, except for the eastern hillock, there was simply not sufficient or appropriate land for constructing the university buildings. Moreover, any future expansion would be virtually impossible without destroying the forest area (natural park) from where one can see beautiful views of snow-capped peaks to the north.

Finally, in the evening of 31 July 1988, all the stakeholders were summoned to the Royal Palace to discuss the issue in the presence of their Majesties. Also present were Minister K.B. Bista, Secretary Mr. N.N. Singh, Dr. Sharma, and palace officials Mr. N.P. Shrestha and Mr. S.B. Dongol. Dr. Sharma presented his argument and then I was asked to present mine. My argumentation was seven-fold. Firstly, I argued that the some of the university area lay within the WHS, some in the buffer zone, and some in the forest and natural park. Therefore it would be wrong to grant permission to construct new buildings in that area. Furthermore, even if a building should be necessary, it would have to be constructed according to the norms and conditions specified for the Protected Monument Zone and WHS. Thirdly, the area which had been demarcated for the university was the most strategic area in the Changu Narayan WHS, and was needed for infrastructure development of the site to attract pilgrims in future. Fourthly, the construction of university buildings would destroy the nearby forest, which was thriving. Moreover, a modern university is a growing and ever-expanding institution. It needs plenty of space, and many tall, big buildings might be necessary for its future development – but this WHS could never accept such new structures around it and in its vicinity. Sixthly, as this was a university focused on the natural sciences, it would probably need plenty of water – which is very scarce in this area. And finally, the mediaeval settlement of Changu village represents a further addition to the beauty of this site. Once the university began to develop and grow, the mounting increase in population would be very harmful and could certainly create disturbances in the lives of the villagers. It might damage and disturb their cultural harmony as well as their traditional identity. Therefore an institution like a modern university should go to an area that can provide ample scope for expansion.

After my presentation, their Majesties did not say anything, but they and all the others had been listening very attentively. A few days later, I was informed that the Palace had requested Dr. Sharma to find another suitable site for the university. And thus Kathmandu University came to have its present location at Banepa, further to the east, near the Valley rim.

According to the same newspaper report mentioned elsewhere in this book, in Changu Narayan Monument Zone there were, as of spring 2000, seven houses built against the norms prescribed by the DOA and 24 built without any proper documents. *(Gorakhapatra,* 25Chaitra, BS 2058). Development and modernization have slowly been making inroads, also in the minds of the local people. After the site was declared a World Heritage Site, tourism began to flourish in this small village. To cater to pilgrims and visitors, in recent years souvenir shops and eating-places have begun to spring up. The ancient agricultural village is in the process of becoming a commercial small town, indirectly compelling the residents to change their beautiful little houses into business ventures. This may be unavoidable – but they should never compromise and change the architecture of these old traditional buildings. Instead they should try to amalgamate and adapt their businesses, siting them in their old-style houses – a strategy which is also certain to attract appreciative visitors.

Main façade of Changu Narayan Temple

Changu Narayan Temple from the east (Courtesy: Department of Archaeology)

10

Restoration of Keshar Mahal: Garden of Dreams

We know very little about the garden tradition in Nepalese architecture. Only a few inscriptions from the Lichchavi period mention *Mul Batika Grama*, which translates as 'the village belonging to the main garden' or 'the village situated in the main garden'. One such inscription, dated NS 48 (AD 624), is placed at the temple of Chhinna Masta Devi near Patan Durbar. In another inscription, dated NS 137 (AD 713) and located at Chaysal Tole, Patan, the words *Puspa Batika Vihar* occur, meaning 'the monastery of Puspa Batika (Garden)'.

It is very difficult to believe that Lichchavi palaces like Managriha, Kailashkuta Bhawan, Bhadradibash and Daksin Rajkula had no gardens. Numerous Lichchavi inscriptions and the Tang Annals describe the architectural grandeur of the Kailashkuta Bhawan, but, oddly enough, there is no mention of the gardens of this beautiful palace.

Excavation is the only means to prove the remains of the ancient architecture of any civilization. As yet, however, we have not been able to uncover the ruins of these ancient palaces, even after major excavations in parts of the Kathmandu Valley.

We can, however, assume that there was a Lichchavi tradition of garden culture and that it continued during the mediaeval period. All three Malla palaces of the Kathmandu Valley have gardens known as *bhandarkhal bagiacha* or 'gardens located behind the palace'. There are inscriptions to prove that the Malla kings of the Valley continued the practice of donating land to the temples, for the cultivation of flowers and fruit trees. At the temple of Bringareshwar Mahadev, an inscription from King Shiva Singh of Patan dated NS 734 (AD 1614) specifies that the king donated land for the cultivation of fruits and flowers for Lord Mahadev (Shiva). And King Shidhi Nara Shima Malla's inscription at Patan Bhandarkhal states that in 1647 the king had a pond, a stone waterspout and a flower garden constructed, which he donated in honour of his family deity. The court poet Kunu Sharma, describing the achievements of King Sri Niwas Malla in his famous work 'Kriti Pataka' (1652), writes that in the pond of the Pukhula Baigahicha, 'the yellow lotus flowers are blooming. On all sides of the pond different types of colourful flowers are growing. Fish and tortoises are swimming. On one side there exists a stone spout. Various types of aquatic birds play in the pond, as in [the sacred Tibetan lake of] Kailash Manasorobar.'

King Pratap Malla of Kathmandu had many beautiful stone sculptures brought to decorate the *bhandarkhal* garden of Hanuman Dhokha Palace. In all three *bhandarkhal* gardens of the Kathmandu Valley, ponds and waterspouts were constructed. Unfortunately, these historical gardens have not been maintained or preserved. Reviving them would certainly add to the beauty of these ancient palaces.

According to historian H. Ambrose Oldfield, it was Prime Minister Bhimsen Thapa who introduced European architecture in Nepal in the early decades of the 19th century. His palaces at Chawani, which now house the National Museum, and the Bagh Durbar near Dharahara have been totally altered, however, and their once-beautiful gardens totally destroyed. After his tragic death and also after the death of his nephew Prime Minister Mathabar Singh (who had lived in Bagh Durbar for a short while), the flower gardens were neglected, the fish ponds were left untended, the fountains were left to dry up, the whole area was soon turned into a wilderness (Oldfield, 1880/1974, pp. 108–109).

We do not have any information on the gardens of the famous Thapathali Durbar of Prime Minister Jung Bahadur. Since there were facilities for viewing animal fights and various animal games, there most probably were gardens as well. But no traces remain.

Among the brothers of Jung Bahadur, Bir Shumsher was a great builder. He constructed eight palaces for his sons and brothers. He had Narayanhiti Durbar built for his brother Ranaudip Singh, who later became Prime Minister; his other palaces were Fohara Durbar, Seto Durbar, Lal Durbar, Char Burja or Bahdur Bhawan, Subarna Bhawan, Toran Bhawan and Ananda Niketan. All these palaces had beautiful gardens, with those of Fohara Durbar, Lal Durbar and Seto Durbar being particularly esteemed.

After Bir Shumsher, his brother and Prime Minister, Bhim Shumsher, also had numerous palaces constructed for himself and his wives. Bisal Nagar Durbar, Satya Bhawan, Tangal Durbar, Sita Bhawan, and Baluwatar Durbar or Subarna Mahal were prominent among them. Bisal Nagar Durbar was once famous for its gardens, ponds, statues and trees, and Satya Bhawan was renowned for its orchids. At present only a part of the gardens of Subarna Mahal (now owned by the Nepal National Bank) can be seen.

Rana Prime Minister Chandra Shumsher had Singha Durbar built as the official residence of the Rana prime ministers. He also had numerous palaces built for his sons – Sital Niwas, Laxmi Niwas, Saha Mahal, Keshar Mahal, Babar Mahal, Singha Mahal, Sri Mahal, Harihar Bhawan and other palaces. Luckily, at some of these, the gardens are still maintained – to a degree at least. This is the case at Sital Niwas, Laxmi Niwas, Singha Durbar and Singha Mahal, thanks to the offices and hotels currently occupying these premises (Amatya, 2002a).

Of all the gardens of the Rana era, the Keshar Mahal, or Garden of Dreams (Swapna) was among the most beautiful and most famed. The creator of this garden, Field Marshal Keshar Shumsher Jung Bahadur Rana (1892–1964), son of Prime Minister Chandra Shumsher, was a diplomat – but also a traveller, a connoisseur, a scholar and a great lover of beauty, nature and gardens. In its prime, the Keshar Mahal Garden was one of the finest in Kathmandu, with a rich collection of plants, both exotic and endemic. It was made both beautiful and useful by the construction of six pavilions one for each of the six seasons of the Nepali year.

When I saw this garden in 1968 it was not well maintained. After the death of Keshar Shumsher in 1964 it seemed that his descendants did not give sufficient attention to the garden, and it had already started deteriorating. I noted the abundant growth of wild grasses and poor maintenance of the six pavilions, although traces of the original shape of the garden remained. His family soon sold off a large portion of the garden to private builders. In this part of the garden there had been three beautiful pavilions – *Sharad* (early autumn), *Hemanta* (late autumn) and *Shisir* (winter). These were torn down and destroyed by the new owners. In 1968 the Keshar Mahal, its library and the Dream Garden, with only three dilapidated pavilions remaining – *Basanta* (spring), *Grishma* (early summer) and *Barkha* (monsoon) – was transferred to the Ministry of Education and Culture, Department of Archaeology.

In July 1992, when the renowned botanist Dr. Dibva Dev Bhatt visited the garden, he was greatly disappointed to find it in a state of decay and negligence. 'The paths were littered with the droppings of the egrets which roost on the trees. The ponds were dry and the Pavilions are overgrown with weeds. It was indeed, a gloomy sight. Many trees remain but require care' (Bhatt, 1992).

The adjacent Keshar Mahal Palace was built in 1895. Only in 1908, when it was purchased and given to Keshar Shumsher by his father Prime Minister Chandra Shumsher, was it named Keshar Mahal. The garden is a later addition. According to tradition, Keshar Shumsher constructed it after his numerous visits in Europe and his return from the Court of St. James in London. It is said that the architect planners of the garden were the pioneering engineers of Nepal, the Narasingh brothers. Without doubt, it was inspired by many of the famous historical gardens of Europe.

Tradition goes on to relate what happened to Keshar Shumsher one autumn day during the Tihar festival. It was the feast of Laxmi Puja, the day all when Nepalese like to gamble. Keshar Shumsher, it is said, was gambling with his father, the then Prime Minister Chandra Shumsher, and won a fortune in the game of cowries. Overjoyed at luck, Keshar dedicate a statue to the goddess Laxmi in the garden, which he could then further expand and decorate. Today this statue has been repaired and stands in front of the *Barkha* pavilion.

Field Marshal Keshar Shumsher was a legend of his time. His bronze bust placed in front of the main palace and the similar bronze statue of Lord Krishna next to it have many romantic and interesting stories to reveal. He compared himself to two other great lovers of history – Lord Krishna and Count Casanova. It is said that he had in his palace many young maidservants (sometimes their number goes up to three hundred) to serve his insatiable carnal desires. There was a pavilion in the north side of the garden paved with beautiful Italian marbles. It is said that Keshar Shumsher used to come there with maidservants and tell them to undress. Then he would throw silver coins on the marble floor and the girls were to grab as many as possible. Wrestling tussles ensued, much to his enjoyment.

But this legendary Garden of Dreams was to become the victim of utter negligence and the ravages of time.

After the devastating fire at Singha Durbar in 1975, the Ministry of Education was shifted to this palace, and the sad plight of this palace and the garden began. The *Shisir* or 'Winter Pavilion' was lost when the western part of the original garden was sold and developed into what is now part of Thamel. Two other pavilions – *Hemanta* and *Sharad* – were also lost when much of the garden was sold before handing over what was left to the government. Some three decades of lack of proper maintenance and lack of love for the garden turned the remaining area into a wasteland, or rather a big open dustbin.

Then, one fine morning during Visit Nepal Year 1998, Karna Sakya, the Convenor of the National Co-ordination Committee of Visit Nepal Year, noticed that workers were tearing off the southern roof of the Barkha pavilion in the garden. Deeply shocked, he immediately approached the Ministry of Education to stop this activity, and also requested the intervention of the Nepal Heritage Society and the Department of Archaeology. One year earlier, some garden lovers, both Nepalese and foreigners, had approached the Austrian Foreign Minister Ms. Benita Ferreo-Waldner, who was in Nepal to attain the inauguration ceremony of the newly completed Patan Museum, for her co-operation in rescuing this garden. As a result of her promise to help Karna Shakya, Lok Bhakta Rana, Gotz Hagmuller and myself as Acting Director-General of the Department of Archaeology took the initiative. A bilateral project between Austria and Nepal was to be the result.

In this effort, Nepalese and expatriates have been working closely together, with the financial and technical assistance of the federal government of Austria. This unique joint venture project is intended to give to the Garden of Dreams a new lease of life. Though what remains of the garden is not even half of its original size, three of its grand neo-classical pavilions, central lotus pond and most of the other architectural and sculptural elements have survived, and have now been restored and conserved. We are hopeful that the revival of this garden can inspire the restoration of other historical gardens in Nepal.

On 30 January 2002, a six-year agreement was signed between the Ministry of Education and Sports, His Majesty's Government of Nepal and the Federal Minister for Foreign Affairs of the Republic of Austria, on 'The Historic Preservation and Development of Educational, Natural and Cultural Resources of the Swapna Garden, Keshar Mahal'. In accordance with the agreement, HMG, Ministry of Education established 'The Swapna Garden Development Board' (SGDB) under the chairmanship of the Secretary of the Ministry of Education. After the handover of the completed project, SGDB will have full responsibility for preparing the annual budget and programmes, preparing and implementing the Master Plan for the development and conservation of the Swapna Garden, further developing the garden from touristic, environmental and aesthetic perspective, and carrying out income-generating programmes to ensure future development, conservation and maintenance.

Project implementation has been carried out by the Austria-based INGO Eco Himal (under the Austrian Development Co-operation), which has been assisting Nepal in a range of cultural co-operation and heritage conservation projects. For the past seven years, Eco Himal has been involved in the restoration of the Keshar Mahal Garden of Dreams. The main dreamer, planner and architect restorer of this unique project was Prof. Gotz Hagmuller. He has been assisted by Ludmilla Hungerhuber, architect Prajwal Thapa, architect Sirish Bhatt, manager Suresh Shrestha and Suraj Shrestha.

This is the first full-scale eco-cultural tourism project in Nepal of its kind. The project will give Nepalese and tourists a quiet green oasis with flowers, trees and fresh air in the centre of the city.

The main cultural and environmental aims are to rehabilitate the Keshar Mahal Gardens as a part of Nepal's cultural heritage, to restore the architectural, aquatic and landscaping features, and to conserve their unique environmental qualities in the heart of

Kathmandu. At the same time, the project aims at quality tourism development: parts of the gardens are to be utilized for the establishment of high-standard tourist facilities. The plan has been to restore the physical premises of the historic garden while introducing state-of-the-art adaptive re-use design to house a garden café, a fully equipped restaurant and a lounge bar. The basic infrastructure is to be established for such purposes, and subsequent private investment will be invited.

The new main entrance and ticket counter are located just opposite the SAARC Secretariat on the main approach to Thamel. Next to this gate, one of the three remaining garden pavilions, *Grishma,* dedicated to the hot early-summer season, will probably serve as an information centre for quality tourism.

The impressive *Basanta* (spring) Pavilion enjoys a prominent location on the eastern perimeter. It will be converted into the main salon of a café of international character and standard. In front of this pavilion, the restoration of a large ornamental pool studded with beautiful lotus flowers has been completed. In the Southeast corner of the Basanta Pavilion, a restaurant and kitchen wing have been developed.

The *Barkha* (monsoon season) Pavilion will have a lounge bar. A small reflecting pond has been added in front of the Laxmi statue, which stands in front of this pavilion. Some say that originally this was a statue of Nike, the Greek goddess of victory, and that the statue was later remodelled, and then dedicated to the Hindu goddess Laxmi. This re-dedication as Laxmi by Keshar Shumsher is said to have been in gratitude to the goddess of fortune for having provided the means to create the Garden of Dreams in the early 1920s. The complete restoration of the statue, which had lost its head and both hands during the long years of neglect, retains the physical power of Nike, while the lotus she carries and the coins spilling from her other hand are symbols of Laxmi's purity and divine kindness. (See presentation in 'Garden of Dreams', *ECS,* 2007)

A large portion of the garden on the western side is to be maintained as a green area where garden parties, cocktail gatherings, dinners and cultural shows can be arranged. Its beauty is enhanced by the Greek-style rotunda, which can be used for multi-functional purposes. The round table in the middle of the rotunda is surrounded by iron benches and a hanging light. In-between the Basanta Pavilion and the Grishma Pavilion, the large sunken portion of the original garden has now been remodelled to create an impressive open-air amphitheatre for cultural events.

The Keshar Wing houses the main office building. Its ground floor backroom has been converted into a gallery for temporary exhibitions, and a kitchenette has been installed on the first floor. To the west of the Keshar Wing lies the Asade Char Bagh portion of the garden, with its beautiful flowers and shrubbery. Benches and resting places *(chautaras)* have been placed there for the comfort of visitors.

After completion of construction work in the North Service Area, storage, staff rooms, lockers, and other necessary logistics space will be provided. The upper portions will be turned into a viewing terrace.

This restoration of the garden from a private property to a park-garden for the general public also includes some innovative new features that blend into its historic ambience perfectly. Several pools, basins and fountains have been added (originally there was only one pond), and a new open-air theatre has been created for cultural performances and public or private events that now can be hosted on payment. (See Singh & Thapa, 2006.)

The Keshar Mahal Garden of Dreams Restoration and Tourism Development Project had a 'soft opening' in October 2006, with concerts and other cultural events. Since then many visitors have come to enjoy the peace and quiet of this historic garden. Numerous social and cultural events have already been organized. (See e.g. Amatya, 2002b).

It is indeed to be hoped that the revival of this garden will open our eyes and inspire us to revive other historical gardens of Nepal. Keshar Shumsher himself had placed an inscription with some verses from the famous *Rubaiyat* of Omar Khayyam by the Basanta Pavilion:

> *Ah, Moon of my Delight who know'st no wane,*
> *The Moon of Heav'n is rising once again:*
> *How oft hereafter rising shall she look*
> *Through this same Garden after me --in vain!*
>
> - But now we know that this garden shall not go in vain: it is to remain for years to come, thanks to Eco Himal and the unique bilateral project between Austria and Nepal.

A bilateral project between Austria and Nepal implemented by the INGO Eco Himal (Austrian Development Cooperation), which has been assisting Nepal in various Cultural Cooperation and Heritage Conservation Projects. Since last seven years Eco Himal has been involved in the restoration of the Keshar Mahal Garden of Dreams. The main dreamer, planner and architect restorer of this project was Prof. Gotz Hagmuller. He was assisted by Ludmilla Hungerhuber, architect Prajwal Thapa, architect Sirish Bhatt, manager Suresh Shrestha and Suraj Shrestha.

Main (northern) entrance of Dream Garden: Keshar Mahal before renovation

Main (northern) entrance of Dream Garden: Keshar Mahal after renovation

Basanta Pavilion before renovation

Basanta Pavilion after renovation

Round steps and the large sunken portion before renovation

Round steps and the large sunken portion after renovation

Western side of the garden before renovation

Western side of the garden after renovation

Balustrade on the eastern side of the garden before renovation

Balustrade on the eastern side of the garden after renovation with a gate

Lotus pond before renovation

Lotus pond after renovation

Stucco image of Nike/Goddess Laxmi before restoration

Stucco image of Nike/Goddess Laxmi after restoration

Pergola from the east to the west before renovation

Pergola from the east to the west after renovation

11

Conclusion: Thoughts on Heritage, Area-Based Conservation, and the Future

The cultural heritage of the Kathmandu Valley is facing many challenges from various aspects of today's pseudo-modern life. The threats come from nature, from time and from human beings. So extreme is the fragility and vulnerability of the Valley's cultural heritage that every year many important monuments either collapse or are defaced or encroached on. Above all, it is essential today that our society, our people and we as individuals should recognize that this cultural heritage, handed down to us by our ancestors, is our most precious asset. Our country is known to the outside world because of the values and uniqueness of this heritage. If we fail to preserve and protect it, we will lose our identity as well as our validity.

We need to protect, preserve and share our cultural heritage with the entire world. It is aptly said: what *is even more important is the realization that there cannot be a cultural heritage for mankind unless it exists in the mind of man*. The cultural heritage of the Kathmandu Valley is a truly universal heritage that extends beyond man-made frontiers. The whole world should therefore be involved in ensuring its protection. We, the present generation, are responsible for prolonging the life of our heritage, our monuments, and protecting the built environment of our historic cities so that future generations can enjoy them profitably. We are here as the custodians of our children's heritage. If we can successfully preserve this heritage, we will be remembered in future by our children. Otherwise we will be forgotten by them, just as the pages of a history book may be read and then ignored (Amatya, 1993a).

After the catastrophic earthquake of 1934, many new building materials – cement, iron beam, marble and corrugated metal sheets – were introduced, bringing massive changes to traditional Nepalese architecture. After the restoration of the monarchy in 1950–51, the freedom to travel to India gave more opportunities for wealthy Nepalese to introduce new building materials and designs in constructing their buildings. After the 1960s, the people of the Valley began to replace their traditional roof tiles *(*or *jingitis)* with corrugated metal sheets, which are easy to maintain. They also began to cover the façades of their brick houses with cement, thinking it would help to protect the walls from heavy rains. By the 1970s, numerous old houses had been demolished and replaced by ugly new box-like constructions of cement. When the Kathmandu Valley was declared a UNESCO World Heritage Site 1979, it was hoped that this would help to save the ancient architectural heritage of the Valley.

During my childhood, my parents had impressed on me that we should not build our houses higher than the pinnacle of the nearest religious structure – whether that was a temple or a monastery or a stupa or a *deo chhen* (god-house shrine). Indeed, for many centuries nobody ventured to disobey this unwritten law or belief. But as time passed, the people began to forget the old values. After the 1960s we saw our neighbours constructing their houses much larger, bigger and taller than the nearby adjoining religious buildings. There are many reasons why people are disregarding their traditional beliefs and values. The first and foremost is that they have embraced a materialistic approach towards life. This new approach has changed not only their lifestyle but also the entire environment – and this includes the architectural heritage of our country and the morphology of our urban space. In fact, by the 1980s, the environment of these heritage sites had deteriorated so much that it seemed impossible to rectify things.

Despite decades of accelerating re-development and change, the Kathmandu Valley still has palaces and temples, the old pattern of streets and courtyards, and many traditional houses. But every year sees more of that historic fabric lost. Today's race towards complete re-development should be stopped immediately – or at least be properly controlled, in line with acceptable heritage conservation policy. Control with maximum building heights, plot coverage, design guidelines, architectural relationship to historic buildings, and demolition activities should be strictly enforced, as detailed in the Heritage Regulations. Here let me point out how important is the role that our municipalities, wards and local administration have to play in fulfilling these tasks.

The general conservation policy should be to protect, conserve and restore areas of historic, aesthetic, architectural, social, cultural or archaeological importance, as well as to guide their development and harmonious adaptation to contemporary life. The point is not to create a museum environment, but to upgrade historic areas within a vibrant, living city.

The preservation of historic towns and historic districts or areas must be an integral part of every community's comprehensive planning process. All planning efforts – plans for land use, economic development, housing, public utilities and facilities, transportation, recreation, housing and social services, open space and urban design – must incorporate historical preservation goals if they are to serve the needs of local inhabitants. This is also true of national, state, and regional planning efforts having a direct effect on local areas. (US/ICOMOS 1992)

Moreover, Article 1 of the Venice Charter states: *the concept of an historic monument embraces not only the single architectural work, but also the urban or rural setting in which is found the evidence of a particular civilization, a significant development or an historic event*.

Area-based conservation means that a place – and not just individual monuments – is recognized as being important to the community, for historical, cultural or architectural reasons. All the usual planning activities – infrastructure upgrading, traffic management, environmental improvements, land use, development control etc. – are informed by the primary objective of conserving and improving the essential character of that place. The conservation area does not become a sterile museum piece, but remains part of the living city. The city continues to change and evolve, as cities have always done, but change is managed to prevent the destruction of the historic character.

Area conservation means that not only palaces and temples, but also streets and houses, are all recognized as part of the cultural heritage. If all the old houses are re-developed, Kathmandu will no longer be an historic city. In many parts of the world, old buildings have come to be recognized as a valuable resource, in economic as well as cultural terms. It is a mistake to think that conservation is a luxury which can be afforded only by rich Western societies. Conservation is an attitude to the careful use of limited resources, applicable to many aspects of the environment as well as the built heritage. And historic houses are a very limited resource: once they are gone, they cannot be recovered.

Merely placing restrictions on the building activities of the local people is not enough, if we are to succeed in preserving the cultural and natural environment. The government should try to fulfil the people's desires and aspirations to see something specific, the results of development activities on the site itself. The government should immediately launch high-profile activities like the restoration of monuments, reforestation, removal of visual impairments, the development of facilities and infrastructures, etc. Once the local people have become convinced that the government is really serious and committed to the forward-looking development of the area, then it would not be difficult to mobilize them and materialize the objectives of area conservation.

Heritage is an essential force of every society. We can change our environment, but not our heritage. Monuments were once a dominant feature of cities of the Kathmandu Valley: indeed, they were considered as temple towns, or towns of monuments. Kathmandu was famed for having more temples than houses, and more gods and goddesses than people. Until only a few decades ago, these monuments dominated the whole environment of the Valley. Changes over the past four or five decades have altered everything. Ancient temples are overshadowed by multi-storeyed concrete matchbox buildings. Cable television, satellite dishes and massive wiring have further damaged the skyscape of these cities. Neglect in timely repair and maintenance of our monuments, the decline in use of these edifices, and the alienation of people from their own heritage have not only affected public morality but also worsened our living conditions.

The cultural heritage of the Kathmandu Valley has an intimate relationship with the daily life of the people. There was a time when they would get up every morning to the sound of the temple bells. How can we save the Valley from all the many hazards it faces? How can we develop it with discipline and regulation? How can we make it free from the many types of pollution? How can we protect, preserve and utilize our heritage? How can we maintain the Valley as the cultural capital of our nation?

Everything is culture. Everything that depends on human beings or has been influenced by them is culture. For this reason, culture is also an important component of development policy. It is important to preserve the cultural diversity and identity of the world's different peoples in the face of increasing globalization. And here, the most important thing is the people's will and interest to protect and preserve their heritage. If the people themselves are not willing to save their heritage, no one can help them. The government is only a vehicle to carry their will and their interests. People should accept that the government is not placing unnecessary restrictions on their building activities, but that, through such discipline, it seeks to guide them onto the right path and save their own property, their ancestral heritage, for their own benefit and for future generations.

Confrontations have taken place between the people and the government, due to sheer misunderstanding and lack of proper knowledge. If this persists, our architectural heritage is likely to be the loser. The destruction caused will be so much that we will not need any new natural calamity or bombardment. Then whom shall we blame – the government, or we the people ourselves? Therefore, the government, together with various NGOs and competent individuals, should arouse awareness among the people for heritage protection, working hand in hand for heritage conservation. Heritage conservation awareness among the people is essential. To create it, all stakeholders need to work together – and this extends to the relevant government agencies, political parties, elites of society and various NGOs working for heritage conservation.

The decision made by the government in April 1993 to demolish more than 1200 houses in Kathmandu, Patan and Bhaktapur Municipal areas, built against the existing laws or building codes, has yet to be implemented. The government has issued warnings to illegal builders, but no one has heeded them. Such failures on the part of the authorities in executing their decisions have not only boosted the morale of illegal builders, but also encouraged others also to commit such crimes.

Here comes the role of the local leaders in preserving our built heritage. The local leaders should bear in mind that every piece of built heritage is not only their precious property but also a prestigious and glorious part of our built environment. By 'built heritage' is meant not only the historically, artistically and architecturally rich buildings, monuments and structures, but also the streets, city corners or squares and clusters of houses that comprise the urban morphology. When our ancestors built the three main cities and the smaller towns of the Valley, they did this with a sound knowledge of scientific urban planning. Houses were built in two horizontal lines running along with the streets. The monotonous street lines were broken every two or three minutes of walking time by squares or courtyards, with stone waterspouts, *dabalis* (open platforms), shrines and so on. In these squares, religious structures were built – temples, rest houses, shrines etc. This was truly good urban planning.

Today, however, at all World Heritage Sites of the Kathmandu Valley, we see that posters and hoardings have been put up, wayside vendors are selling curios and handicrafts, there is graffiti on the walls of the monuments and vandalism – all very acute problems. Ignorance and lack of respect for art and architecture are major factors in destroying what has been preserved for generations. Concerning this reckless vandalism, one author has recently written: 'The point is brought home in full public view in Kathmandu Square where the centrally situated temple [Maju Dewal] that has been renovated very recently now bears chalk marks shrilly shouting the perpetrators' names on the wooden shafts. It makes one wonder what kind of love the perpetrators of the crime are declaring for self or each other by marring what was created out of pure love that has lasted through centuries; only to be defaced today by those who can read and write.' (Amatya, 2007)

Local leaders should be the catalyst in changing people's attitudes to heritage preservation. They should impart to them the knowledge that without this built heritage (or with its mis-management) the Kathmandu Valley will become a worse place to live in. Heritage preservation should be a part of school education, from the primary level and onwards. Above all, politicians at the local and national levels should learn about heritage preservation as a part of their responsibility.

In conclusion, let me offer a list of some basic needs for the protection and conservation of the built heritage of the Kathmandu Valley:

- including Heritage Conservation in the new Constitution as the duty and responsibility of the people and the nation ,
- adequate funding and trained technical manpower in heritage conservation activities, in the annual national budget,
- establishment of a 'Monument and Preservation Trust Fund' for providing incentives to the people. In this basket, substantial amounts should come from the DOA, Tourism Development Board, the municipal authorities (including tourist entry fees to WHS) and hotels and travel agencies.
- quick and effective legal procedures should be made to penalize defaulters or illegal builders, because without a legal basis and strict enforcement of these laws, there can be no hope for improvement in the WHS.
- extensive publicity about the WHS/WHL and increased awareness among the people in general, because without positive public opinion and institutional support, legal action will prove ineffective.
- increased mobilization of international help and assistance in heritage conservation efforts (e.g. German, Austrian, US, French, UN/UNESCO, World Heritage Committee, ICOMOS, and others)
- declaration of awards and prizes and incentives to those who build in accordance with DOA norms in WHS, because without financial or other incentives, public opinion support will be hard to achieve.

- assisting people with necessary technical help, such as preparation of house design, in the WHS and also financial help to purchase traditional materials like roof tiles
- providing loans to potential builders and tax exemption to those who construct their houses totally in accordance with the prescribed norms
- regular monitoring of the availability of traditional building materials like *jingitis*, *surki,* timber and bricks.
- improving the façades of structures already built against DOA norms. Subsidies should be provided up to total cost, if possible, for the preservation of historical façades and or details in their original setting.
- roads, sewerage, drinking water pipes, telephone cables and electric lines should be installed without damaging any structures in the WHS. Proper co-ordination should be established between the various infrastructure development agencies. In many cities elsewhere, more is spent on these infrastructural facilities than on heritage conservation.
- vehicular traffic in the WHS should be regulated and controlled
- finally, and importantly: successful implementation of the joint DOA/UNESCO Integrated Management Plan.

Glossary

Aagan Chchen	Sacred temple house
Amsuverma	King of Nepal Valley, 7th century AD
Baha	Larger Buddhist monastery
Bahi	Small Buddhist monastery
Bares	Buddhist caste group of Kathmandu Valley, popularly known as 'Sakyas'
Betal/Betah	Mount of Bhairav – a gentle kind of demon
Bihara/Vihara	Buddhist monastery of Kathmandu Valley
BS	Bikram Sambat or Bikram Era, began AD 822
Byaghrini/Vyaghini	Tiger-faced guardian goddess.
Chaitya	Newa term for small Buddhist shrine; Buddhist hemispherical structure that does not contain the mortal remains of Buddha or other holy person.
Chaku	Portion of the pinnacle of a Stupa below the Kalash
Chattra	Honourific parasol or umbrella
Jajman	Patron responsible for performing rites and rituals
Chowk	Courtyard
Cudamani/Chudamani	Jewel (atop a religious structure)
Dachi appa	Traditional brick
Dalan	Open space on the ground floor
Darsan	Devotional visit

Deo Chhen	House of family divinity or god, different from a temple, architectural form similar to that of traditional residence.
Dewal/Dega	Temple
Dharmasala	Large rest house for pilgrims
Durbar (Darbar)	Royal court
Fayagna	Small metal wind-bells
Gajura	Pinnacle
Ganga	Goddess of river
Garuda	Mythical man-bird, vehicle of the Lord Vishnu
Gartuki/ Galatuki	'Neck' of a religious structure
Ghat	River bank used for bathing, cremation and purification rituals
Gumba	Tibetan Buddhist monastery (often written *gompa)*
Guthi	Socio-religious association of Newas; also trust property organized for the operation and maintenance of religious and social institutions and functions
Guthiar/Guthiyar	Member of the trust or Guthi
Guthi Samsthan/ 'Undertakings'	Government office in charge of religious endowments
Hadigaon	Ancient locality in the northeast of Kathmandu
Harmika	'Neck' or 'chest' of a religious structure (stupa)
Hiti	Stone waterspout
Jamuna	Sister of Ganga and also goddess of river
Jana Andolan	People's revolution
Jatras	Festivals
Jingiting/Jhingati	Traditional roof tiling
Kalash	Pitcher-like shape on the pinnacle of a religious structure

Lichchavi	Dynasty, ruled Nepal Valley or Nepal Mandala from the beginning of the Christian era to the 9th century.
Ma appa	Large traditional brick
Mahachaitya	Great Stupa: used especially of the Swayambhu Stupa
Malla	Dynasty, ruled Nepal Valley from 14th century to 1769
Matrikas	Mother goddesses
Mudra	Religious hand-gesture or position
Newas	Original inhabitants of Kathmandu Valley
NS	Nepal Sambat/ Nepal Era, started AD 879
Pakha Dali	Eaves beam
Pati	Public rest house
Ropani	Unit of land measure, approx. 509 meters
Sattal	Wayside rest house
Shardul	Mythical winged animal
Sinhini/Simhini	Lion-faced guardian goddess
Tara Deo	Female Buddhist deity
Teliya brick	Traditional floor tiles
Thakuri	Dynasty, ruled Central Nepal 9th-14th centuries
Thyasapu	Manuscript or diary
Toran	Tympanum
Yashi, yasti	Central, ceremonial pole of a stupa

Abbreviations

AMPA	Ancient Monument Preservation Act (Nepal)
BDP	Bhaktapur Development Project
CDO	Chief District Officer
CRC	Campaign Review Committee
DOA	Department of Archaeology (Nepal)
GTZ	German Technical Co-operation *(Deutsche Gesellschaft für Technische Zusammenarbeit)*
KMC	Kathmandu Metropolitan Corporation
KVPT	Kathmandu Valley Preservation Trust
KVWHS	Kathmandu Valley World Heritage Site
LCC	Lalitpur Chamber of Commerce
MNO	Bhaktapur Monument Maintenance Office
NIT	Nippon Institute of Technology
PADT	Pashupati Area Development Trust
PMZ	Protected Monument Zone
WHC	World Heritage Committee (UNESCO)
WHL	World Heritage List (UNESCO)
WHS	World Heritage Site (UNESCO)

Bibliography and References

Amatya, Shaphalya, 1983. *Preserving Our Heritage. Heritage Preservation Tourism for Tomorrow.* Kathmandu: PATA.

Amatya, S., 1991. 'Cultural Heritage', *IUCN, Background Papers: to the National Conservation Strategy for Nepal,* (reviewer: L.S. Bangdel), vol. 1, Kathmandu, pp. 23–65.

Amatya, Shaphalya, 1993a. 'Cultural Heritage of Kathmandu', *Rising Nepal*, 18 November.

Amatya, Shaphalya, 1993b. 'Environment of Hanuman Dhoka Palace Complex', *Rising Nepal,* 11 November.

Amatya, Shaphalya, 1993c. 'Problems in Preserving Swayambhunath', *Sunday Post* (Kathmandu) 5 December .

Amatya, Shaphalya 1994a. 'The Future of Kathmandu Valley', *Kathmandu Post,* 4 October.

Amatya, Shaphalya, 1994b. 'Restoration and Rehabilitation of Hanuman Dhoka Palace', *Kathmandu Post,* 2 January.

Amatya, Shaphalya, 1995. *Regulation Growth: Kathmandu Valley, Culture and Heritage* (Annex 5), IUCN (limited distribution)

Amatya, Shaphalya, 1999. *Art and Culture of Nepal*. New Delhi: Nirala (2nd ed.).

Amatya, Shaphalya, 2000 (BS 2057). Hanumandhoka Chhetrama Nisastra Tatha Sasastra Atikraman, *Nepal Samacharpatra*, 14 Chaitra.

Amatya, Shaphalya, 2001 (BS 2058). *Shree Akash Bhairavnath* (in Nepali), Kathmandu.

Amatya, Shaphalya, 2002a 'Garden Culture Catching Up', *Rising Nepal,* 11 October.

Amatya, Shaphalya 2002b. 'Garden of Dreams Becomes a Reality', *The Himalayan*, 21 April.

Amatya, Shaphalya, 2002c. 'Ke Bhaktapurlai Samskritik Nagarka Rupama Goshana Garnu Parla Ta', *Gorakhapatra,* (BS 2059), Ashar 29.

Amatya, Shaphalya, 2003. 'Bhaktapur: The Cultural Capital of Nepal', *Today,* vol. 22, no. 2, April/June, pp. 20–25.

Amatya, Shaphalya, 2004a. 'Garden Tradition in Nepalese Architecture', *Look Nepal,* vol. 7, no. 1, January/Februrary, pp. 27–30.

Amatya, Shaphalya, 2004b. 'Lalitpur (Patan): The City of Fine Arts and Beauty', *Look Nepal,* vol. 7, no. 3, March, pp. 16–20.

Amatya, Shaphalya, 2004c, 'Swayambhu Mahachaitya: A Most Unique World Heritage Site', *Today,* vol. 23, no. 3, September/October.

Amatya, Shaphalya, 2006. 'Hanuman Dhoka Durbar Complex: Centre of Nepalese Cultural Activities', *Look Nepal,* vol. 9, no. 9, September, pp. 25–28.

Amatya, Sushma, 2007. 'Let not ancient art die: destroying, spoiling national heritage should be declared a criminal offence,' *newsfront,* 11–17 June.

Bajracharya, Gautamvajra, 1967, 'Thaysaphu Ko Itihasik Bhakya' (The Historical Interpretation of a Manuscript), *Purnima,* Nepali, Kathmandu, vol. 4, no. 2, pp. 133–139.

Banerjee, N.R., 1977. 'Principles of the Conservation of Ancient Monuments with Special Reference to Nepal', *Ancient Nepal,* No. 40, July, pp. 17–27.

Banerjee, N.R., 1980. *Nepalese Architecture,* Delhi.

Bhatt, Dibva Dev, 1992. 'Preserving the Gardens of Old Rana Palace', *Rising Nepal,* 17 July.

Coon, Ellen, 2007. 'Wonders of Divinity', *Newsfront* weekly (Kathmandu), June 4–10, p. 6; available online at http://www.digitalhimalaya.com/collections/journals/newsfront/pdf/Newsfront_019.pdf

Cotte, Sabine, 1997. 'Proposal for the Conservation of the 17th-Century Wall Paintings at Sundari Chowk, *Preservation of Patan Durbar Square,* Paris: UNESCO/Japan Trust Fund Project (limited distribution).

Darnal, Prakash, 2005. 'Chabahil Sthita Dando Chaitya Jirnodhar Barey Kehi Charcha', *Ancient Nepal,* no. 159, June.

Dowman, Keith, 1993. *The Great Stupa of Boudhanath: The Tibetan Legend of the Great Stupa*, translated with an introduction, rev. 2nd ed., Kathmandu.

Ehrhard, Franz-Karl, 1989. 'A Renovation of Svayambhunath-Stupa in the 18th Century and its History (according to Tibetan sources)', *Ancient Nepal,* no. 114, October/November, pp. 1–8.

Ehrhard, Franz-Karl, 1990. 'The Stupa of Bodhnath: A Preliminary Analysis of the Written Sources', *Ancient Nepal,* No. 120, October/November, pp. 1–10.

Ehrhard, Franz-Karl, 1991. 'Further Renovation of Svayambhunath Stupa (from the 13th to the 17th centuries)', *Ancient Nepal,* no. 123–125, April/September, pp. 10–20.

'Garden of Dreams', 2007. *ECS* monthly (Kathmandu) January, pp. 60–68.

Gutschow, Niels, 2003. 'Techniques in the Architectural Preservation of Nepal: Thoughts About Diversity in the Repair of Timber Pillars', in Theophile & Gutschow, *The Sulima Pagoda.*

Gutschow, Niels; Gotz Hagmuller, Ramesh Jung Thapa & Shaphalya Amatya, 1989. *Svayambhunath: Conservation Masterplan.* Kathmandu: GTZ.

Gutschow, Niels & Gotz Hagmuller, 1991. 'The Reconstruction of the Eight-Cornered Pavilion (Cyasilin Mandap) on Darbar Square in Bhaktapur-Nepal', *Ancient Nepal*, No. 123–125, April/September, pp. 1–10.

Hagmuller, Gotz, 1997. 'Restoration of Patan Museum', *Architecture Design,* September/October, pp. 112–118.

Harrison, John, 2001. *Kathmandu Valley Mapping Programme: Historic Conservation Policy* (Final Report), Kathmandu Metropolitan City/ European Commission.

Joshi, Hari Ram, BS 2030. *Nepalko Prachin Abilekh,* Kathmandu.

Joshi, Ramananda, 1983, (BS 2040) 'Lalitpurko Itihasik Kot-Tahaphaley', *Gorkhapatra*, & also letters to the editor.

Kathmandu Valley Preservation Trust, The Kathmandu Durbar Initiative 2000-2003, Kathmandu, March 2000, Limited distribution.

Kathmandu Valley Preservation Trust, 2002, in co-operation with HMG Department of Archaeology, *Ayu Guthi Sattal: Patan Darbar Square World Heritage Site* (Final Report 2002).

Khanal, Mohan Prasad, 1983 (BS 2040). *Changu Narayanko Itihasik Samagri*, Kathmandu.

Koirala, Kulchandra, BS 2051. *Nepalka Aradhya Deva Bhagwan Shree Pashupatinath,* Kathmandu.

Kolver, Bernhard, 1992. *Re-Building a Stupa: Architectural Drawings of the Svayambhunath.* Bonn: VGH Wissenschaftsverlag.

Manandhar, Razen, 2007. 'Nepal Urged to Seek Inclusion of More Heritage Sites in UNECO List', *The Himalayan Times,* 17 June (http://www.thehimalayantimes.com/Archive.asp).

Manandhar, Sarala, 2000. 'I Baha Bahi: A Buddhist Monastery', *Ancient Nepal*, No. 144, March, pp. 1–12.

Munakarmi, Lila Bhakta, 1984 (BS 2041) *Nepalako Samskritik Tatha Itihasik Digdarshan,* Bhaktapur.

Munakarmi, Lila Bhakta, 2001 (BS 2058). *Mallaka Kriti Ra Abhilekhaharu,* Bhaktapur.

Nepal, H.M. Government of, Ministry of Education and Culture, Department of Archaeology, 1992. *Patan Durbar Samrakshit Smarak Chetra: Ek Parichaya,* Kathmandu (limited distribution).

Nepal, H.M. Government of, & UNESCO, 1975. *Kathmandu Valley, the Preservation of Physical Environment and Cultural Heritage, A Protective Inventory,* Vienna: Schroll.

Oldfield, H. Ambrose, 1880/1974. *Sketches from Nepal,* 2 vols (reprinted Delhi: Cosmo).

Parajuli, Yogeshwas K., 1986. *Bhaktapur Development Project: Experience In Preservation and Restoration in a Medieval Town (1974–1985),* with introductory chapters by S. Amatya & K. Sturzbecher. Kathmandu.

PATA Nepal Chapter & Nepal Heritage Society, 1983. *Heritage Preservation Tourism for Tomorrow,* Kathmandu.

Petech, Luciano, 1984. *Mediaeval History of Nepal*, rev. ed., Rome: Istituto per il Medio ed Estremo Oriente.

Prasai, Surya B. 'Preservation Cultural & Natural Heritage', 1981. *The Rising Nepal,* 1 December, p. 2

Proctor, Giles & Keshav Raj Jha, 2001. *Evaluation: International Safeguarding Campaign for the Kathmandu Valley 979–2001*(limited distribution) Paris/Kathmandu: UNESCO. Text available online at: http://www.buildingconservationservices.com/5.Kathmandu.pdf

Pruscha, Carl (co-ordinator), 1975. *Kathmandu Valley: Preservation of Physical Environment and Cultural Heritage Protective Inventory,* Vol. I, prepared by HMG Nepal in collaboration with the United Nations and UNESCO. Vienna: Anton Schroll & Co.

Rajbamsi, Shankar Man, 1970 (BS 2027). *Kantipur Silalekh Suchi, Rastriya Abhilekhalaya,* Kathmandu.

Ranjitkar, Rohit K.; Lumanti Joshi & Raju Roka, 2005. *Kageswar Mahdev Temple,* Kathmandu Durbar Initiative, Final Report. Kathmandu: KVPT.

Ranjitkar, Rohit & Raju Roka, 2002. *Indrapur Temple*: Kathmandu Durbar Initiative 2000–2004, Final Report. Kathmandu: KVPT.

Rau, Heimo, 1977, 'The Pujari Matha of the Dattatreya Temple, Bhaktapur, and its Restoration. A Preliminary Report', *Journal of the Nepal Research Centre,* vol. I, pp. 117–129.

Regmi, Jagadish Chandra, 1969 (BS 2026), *Lichchavi Samskriti,* Kathmandu: Ratna Pustak Bhandar.

Regmi, Jagadish Chandra, 1976 (BS 2033). *Shahkalin Kala Ra Vastukala,* Kathmandu.

Sanday, John, 1978. *Building Conservation in Nepal: a Handbook of Principles and Techniques,* Paris: UNDP/UNESCO (limited distribution).

Sanday, John, 1979. *Monuments of the Kathmandu Valley.* Paris: UNESCO.

Sanday Kentro Associates 1999, *Patan Heritage Conservation Action Plan* (Master Plan), Lazimpat, Kathmandu.

Sakya, Hem Raj, 1961 (BS 2018). *Kumveshwar Ko Itihas*, Patan.

Sakya, Hem Raj, 1974 (NS 1094) *Manigala Raj Prasad: Patan Durbar Square,* Lalitpur (Patan).

Sakya, Hem Raj, 1978. *Shree Swayambhu Mahachaitya, The Swayambhu Vikas Mandal.* Kathmandu.

Sakya, Hem Raj, 1988 (BS 2045; NS1108) (researcher and editor), *Mahbuddha Mandir: Samchipta Itihas,* Kathmandu.

Sakya, Hem Raj (ed.), 1970 (BS 2027). *Stupa: Samchipta Itihas,* Kathmandu.

Sakya, S. & S. Bhashkaradeva, 2005. *Inscriptions from Itumba/Itumba Abhilekha Sangraha*, Kathmandu:Sri Kesacandra Mahavihara Samrakshana Samaja.

Sekler, Eduard F., 1977. *Master Plan for the Conservation of the Cultural Heritage of the Kathmandu Valley.* Paris: UNESCO.

Sekler, Eduard F., 1980. *Proposal for the Urbanistic Conservation of Patan (Lalitpur) Durbar Square as a Monument Zone,* Harvard Publication Series in Architecture, Cambridge, MA: Harvard University (limited distribution)

Sekler, Eduard F., 1992. 'Changing Concepts of Value in Historic Conservation', Address to GSD alumni, 3 June.

Shrestha, Shobha, 1992. 'Restoration of Viswanath Temple at Patan Durbar Square', *Ancient Nepal,* No. 128–129, February/May, pp. 1–5.

Shrestha, Shreemati Sobha, 1989. 'Bouddhanathko Parichaya, Batavaran Samrakshanma Dekhapareyka Samasya ra Samadhanka Upayaharu', *Ancient Nepal*, no. 110–112, February/July pp. 34–40

Shumsher, Maj. Gen. Brahma, *Nepalko Mahabukampa, 1934* (The Great Earthquake of Nepal, 1934), Kathmandu: Jorganesh Chapakhnana.

Singh, Richa & Shivendra Thapa, 2006. 'Garden of Dreams: A Vintage from a Vantage', *Shangri-la* in-flight magazine, October/December, pp. 57–60).

Slusser, Mary Shepherd, 2005. *Art and Culture of Nepal: Selected Papers.* Kathmandu: Mandala.

Slusser, Mary Shepherd & Gautamavajra Vajracarya, 1974. 'Two Medieval Nepalese Buildings: An Architectural and Cultural Study', *Artibus Asiae,* vol. 36, no. 3, pp. 169–218.

Sullivan, Sharon, 2003. 'Venice, Burra and Kathmandu', in Theophile & Gutschow, *The Sulima Pagoda*.

Suwal, Rajendra Suwal et al., 1979, *Kathmandu Valley Town Planning and Its Impact*. Kathmandu: CEDA, November.

Tamrakar, Tej Ratna, 1989. 'Hanuman Dhoka Durbar Samrakshit Smarak Chetrako Parichaya, Batavaran Samrakshanma Dekha Pareyka Samashya Ra Samadhanaka Upayaharu', *Ancient Nepal,* no. 110–112, February/July, pp. 19–26.

Tandon, Govinda, 1996 (BS 2053). *Pashupati ksetrako Sanskritika Adhayayana*, Kathmandu

Tewari, Ramaji, ed. 1962 (BS 2019), 'Manigalabajara Manimandapako abhilekha (The Manimandapa inscription of Mangal Bazaar)', *Abhilekha- Sangraha,* pt 6 (Kathmandu), pp. 21–22.

Theophile, Erich, 2003. 'The "Art" of Conservation: Subjectivity and Contradictions in an Architect's Conservation Practice', in Theophile & Gutschow, eds, *The Sulima Pagoda*

Theophile, Erich G. & Rohit K. Ranjitkar, 1999. Kathmandu Valley Preservation Trust, in co-operation with HMG Department of Archaeology, Ayu Guthi Sattal: *Patan Darbar Square, Ward 11 (Historic Structure Report, January 1996)* (Limited distribution).

Theophile, Erich & Niels Gutschow, eds, 2003. *The Sulima Pagoda: East Meets West in the Restoration of a Nepalese Temple*, Weatherhill Books, for the Kathmandu Valley Preservation Trust .

UNESCO, Nepal National Commission & Department of Archaeology, 1999. *International Campaign for the Safeguarding of the Cultural Heritage of Kathmandu Valley*, Fourth Meeting of Campaign Review Committee, 14–16 July 1999, Kathmandu. Paris: UNESCO.

UNESCO, Nepal National Commission, 1991. *International Campaign for the Safeguarding of the Kathmandu Valley, Nepal*, Final report of second working group meeting, 10–12 October 1991, Kathmandu (limited distribution).

UNESCO, Kathmandu, 2006, Bhaktapur, Cultural Portraits Handbook, No. 3, p. 17.

US/ICOMOS Specialized National Committee on Historical Towns, 1992. A Preservation Charter for the Historic Towns, adopted by the committee, Fredericksburg, VA, 14 March, proposed for adoption by the board of trustees, US/ICOMOS (printed circular).

Vaidya, Janak Lal, 2004. *Siddhagmi Kotyahuti Dewal Pratistha,* Kathmandu: Nepal Academy.

Vajracharya, Dhanavajra, 1964 (BS 2021), *Chowkvahtha Durbar* (The Four Tower Palace), Purnima (Nepali), Year 1, No. 3, pp. 46-51.

Vajracharya, Dhanavajra, 1973 (BS 2030), *Lichchavi Kalin Abhilekh* (Lichchavi Inscriptions), Kritipur.

Vajracharya, Dhanavajra & Kamal P. Malla, 1985. *The Gopalarajavamsavali,* Kathmandu.

Vajracharya, Gautamvajra, 1976. *Hanuman Dhoka Rajdurbar*, Tribhuwan University, Kathmandu.

'Valley Struck Off UNESCO Endangered Sites' List', 2007. *The Himalayan Times,* 26 June, p.1. (http://www.thehimalayantimes.com/Archive.asp).

Venice Charter: International Charter for the for the Conservation and Restoration of Monuments and Sites, available at http://www.icomos.org/venice_charter.html.

von Rospatt, Alexander, 2001. 'A Historical Overview of the Renovations of the Svayambhucaitya at Kathmandu', *Journal of the Nepal Research Centre*, vol. 12, pp. 195–241.

Wright, Daniel, 1966. *History of Nepal.* Calcutta: Ranjan Gupta (3rd ed).